ultimate Guitar®
CHORD DECODER
THE MOST ESSENTIAL CHORDS FOR ALL GUITAR STYLES

BY JOE CHARUPAKORN

T0061288

To access audio visit:
www.halleonard.com/mylibrary

2120-2691-1338-4376

ISBN 978-1-4584-1818-0

HAL•LEONARD®
CORPORATION
7777 W. Bluemound Rd. P.O. Box 13819 Milwaukee, WI 53213

In Australia Contact:
Hal Leonard Australia Pty. Ltd.
4 Lentara Court
Cheltenham, Victoria, 3192 Australia
Email: ausadmin@halleonard.com.au

Visit Hal Leonard Online at
www.halleonard.com

CONTENTS

ABOUT THE AUTHOR

Joe Charupakorn is a guitarist and best-selling author. He has authored numerous titles including, *Signature Licks: The Best of Yngwie Malmsteen* and *Jazz Improv Basics*, published by Hal Leonard Corporation. He has also interviewed artists like Steve Vai, Joe Satriani, and Tosin Abasi, among many others for *Premier Guitar* magazine. Visit him on the Web at joecharupakorn.com.

ABOUT THE AUDIO

To access the audio examples that accompany this book, simply go to www.halleonard.com/mylibrary and enter the code found on page 1. This will grant you instant access to every example. The examples that include audio are marked with an audio icon throughout the book.

Guitars: Joe Charupakorn

Bass guitar: Chad Johnson

Drums: Chad Johnson

INTRODUCTION

The *Ultimate-Guitar Chord Decoder* is aimed at guitarists who are mystified by chords. While there are many chord books available, a common roadblock is that most of these books just list every possible chord—useful or not—like a dictionary lists every word. With that method, it's easy to become intimidated and frustrated because your energy is spent trying to memorize chord shapes that you might not really need. Instead, you could be focusing on the important chords used most often by the masters. *The Ultimate-Guitar Chord Decoder* displays only the most essential chords that you'll need to have under your fingers in the most practical and useful fingerings, along with an easy-to-understand primer on chord construction. From open position power chords all the way up to advanced altered and extended jazz voicings, you'll have all the chords you'll ever need to use in your lifetime, regardless of what style of music you play.

You can start anywhere you'd like in the book. It doesn't have to be at the beginning. Every moveable chord fingering is shown in all twelve keys using TAB. Therefore, reading standard notation is not required.

The audio tracks are musical examples of what the chords sound like in a typical context. You'll note that certain chord types are better suited for certain styles. Power chords and basic barre chords are the preferred choice for rock, metal and pop, whereas extended and altered chords are the backbone of a jazz musician's harmonic vocabulary. Of course, this doesn't mean that you can't experiment. Jimi Hendrix popularized the use of the jazzy 7♯9 chord in a rock context and since then, the guitar world has never been the same!

READING TAB

Tablature, or TAB, is used for the actual musical examples. Here is an explanation of how to read TAB if you're not already familiar.

Tabulature graphically represents the guitar fingerboard. Each horizontal line represents a string, and each number represents a fret. Rhythmic values are shown using ovals, stems, and dots.

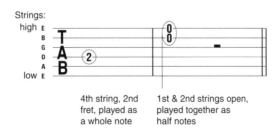

4th string, 2nd fret, played as a whole note

1st & 2nd strings open, played together as half notes

READING CHORD DIAGRAMS

Chord diagrams are a graphic representation of a small portion of the guitar neck and are used to show the note location and fingering of specific chord voicings. The perspective of a chord diagram is as if you are looking at a guitar on a stand in front of you (see the diagram below). The horizontal lines represent frets and the vertical lines represent strings. (Note: The 6th string is the thickest, lowest-sounding string.) Dots indicate where to place your fingers (hollow dots are used to indicate the chords root). To the right of the diagram is a fret marker, which indicates the specific fret the chord is to be played on. The only time you will not see fret markers is in the open-position, where the lowest fret is the first fret and a nut is shown as part of the chord grid. Directly below the diagram are numbers indicating which fingers to use. For guitar:

1 = index

2 = middle

3 = ring

4 = pinky

Occasionaly, the thumb may be used. The thumb is indicated as T. A barre uses one finger to cover more than one string.

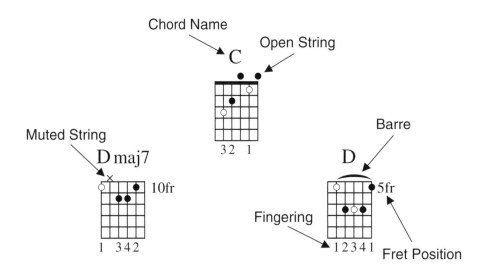

CHOOSING CHORD FINGERINGS

Depending on the context, you may find the need to re-finger chords to suit a particular situation. Here are some general guidelines:

1. Try to minimize finger movement from one chord to the next. If you can keep the same finger on the same note throughout the chord change then do so, otherwise move as little as needed.

2. Always assess the progression and choose a fingering accordingly. What may work for a single isolated chord may not allow for rapid change throughout a progression.

3. Whenever there is stretch involved, use your outer fingers. First finger for stretches toward the headstock and pinkie for stretches toward the bridge.

4. If two or more notes are on the same fret but different strings you may be able to use a barre. (A barre is the straightening of a finger to hold down two or more strings. It is shown in the diagrams as a curved line). The barre should be employed only if it will not obstruct the path of another string being played.

OPEN POSITION ESSENTIAL CHORDS

If you're new to guitar, the *open position essential chords* are the ones you'll want to learn and memorize first. Open position chords are played within the first four frets of the guitar and typically—but not always—contain at least one open string. Included in this section are the most common and important open position chords ranging from full, six string chords, to two note power chords. With these chords, you can cover styles of music from campfire sing-alongs to the heaviest of metal.

Here, the chords are organized by root, so if you're looking for an A or an A minor chord, it will be on the page where the chords built off an A root are. Learn some of the music examples to get a feel for how these chords are typically used and to see which chords go with which.

C Root

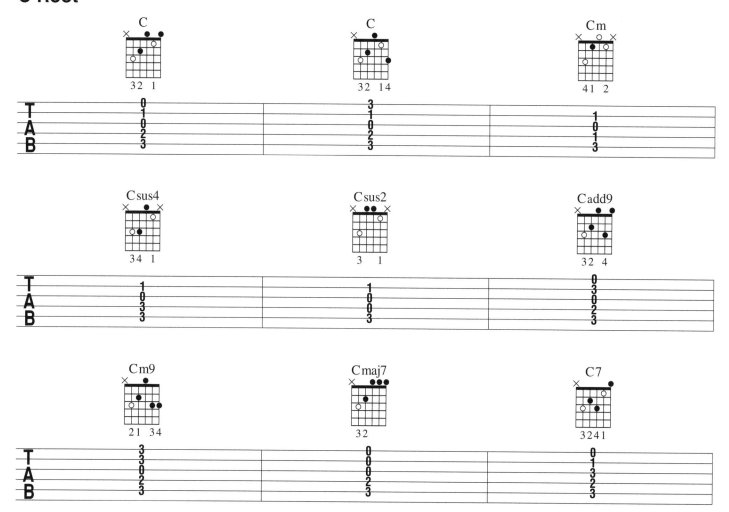

A Root

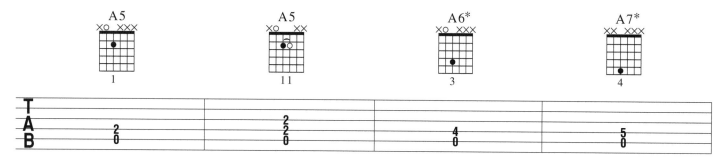

*Because there are no 3rds, these are technically not true A6 and A7 chords.

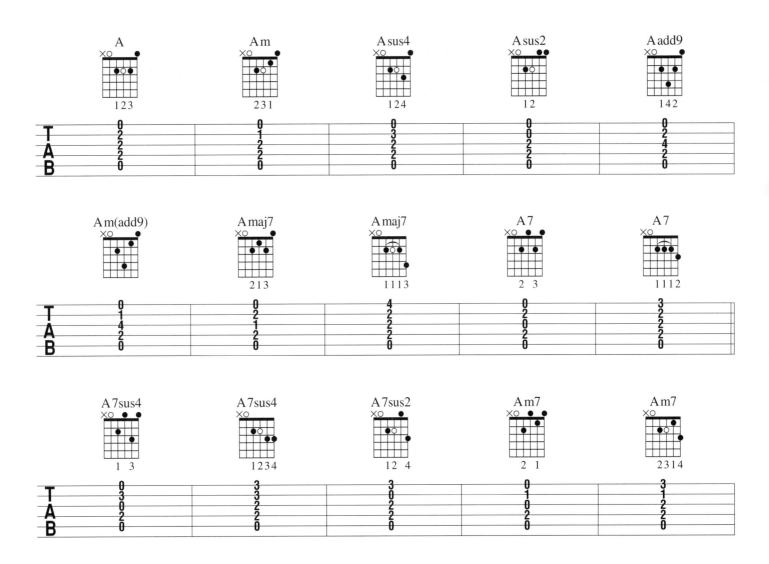

G Root

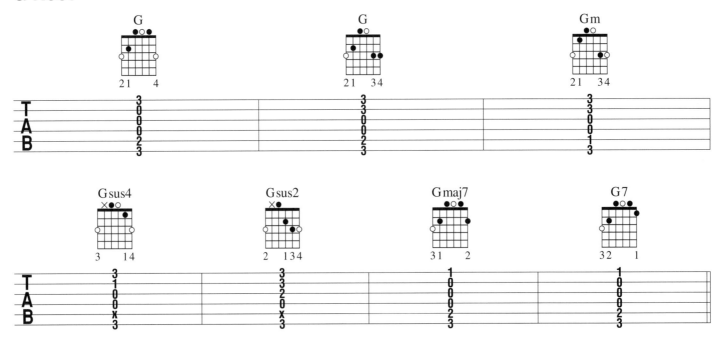

E Root

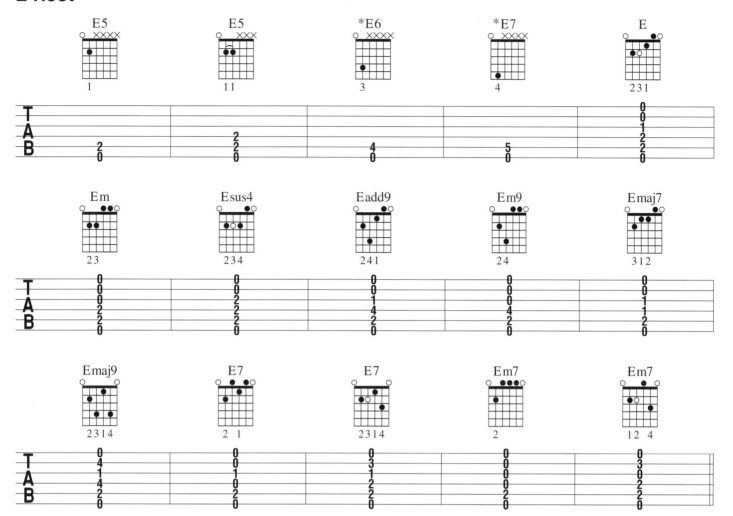

*Because there are no 3rds, these are technically not true E6 and E7 chords.

D Root

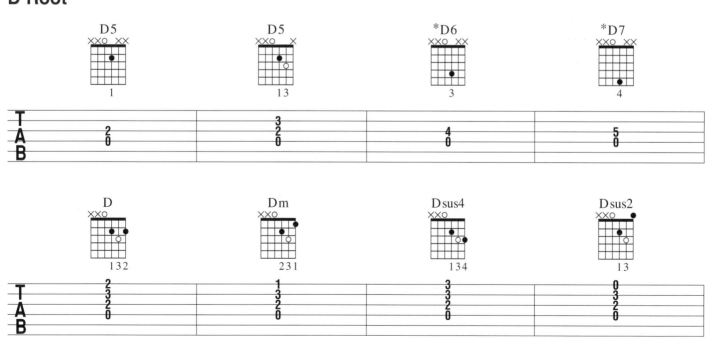

*Because there are no 3rds, these are technically not true D6 and D7 chords.

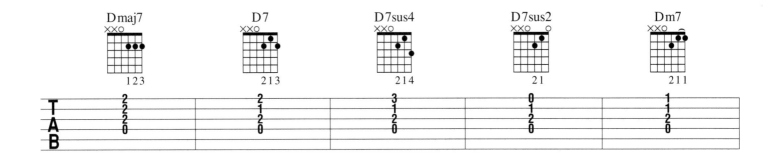

B Root

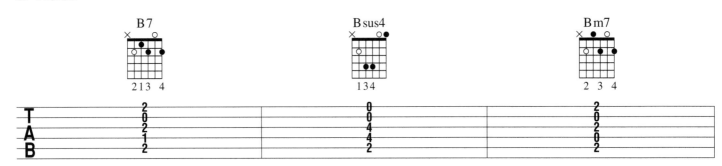

F Root

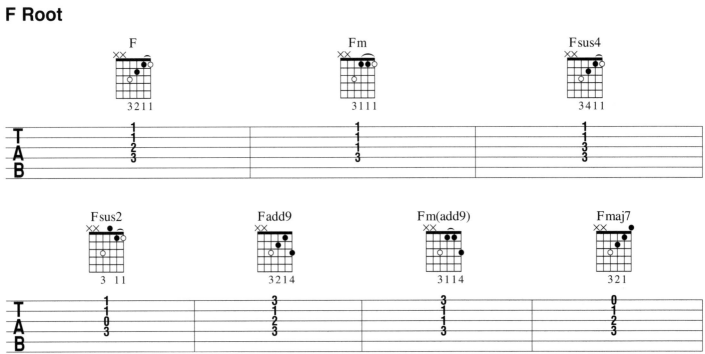

Music Examples

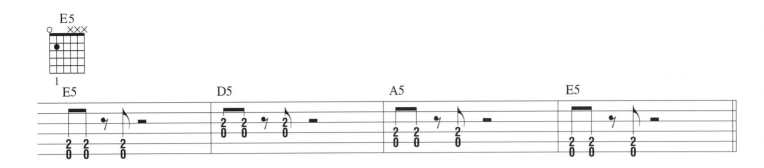

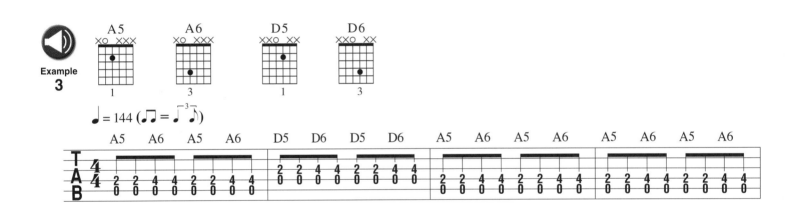

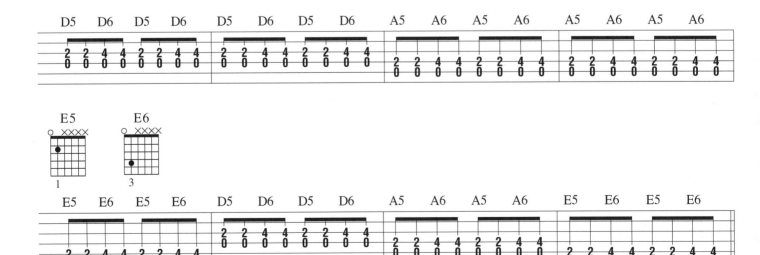

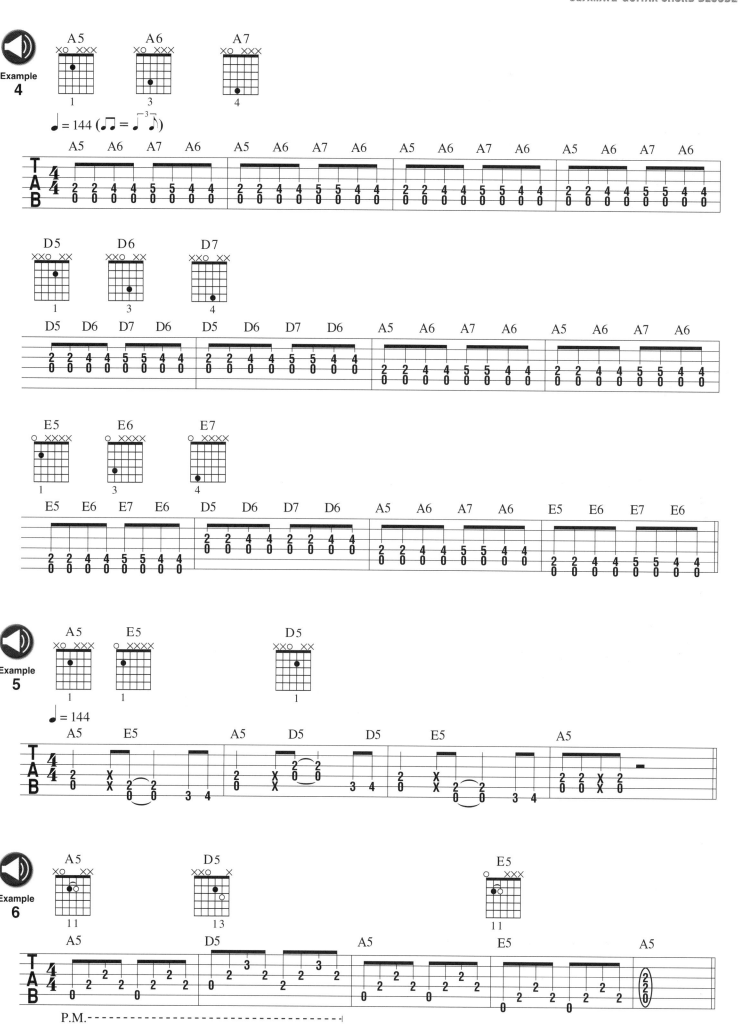

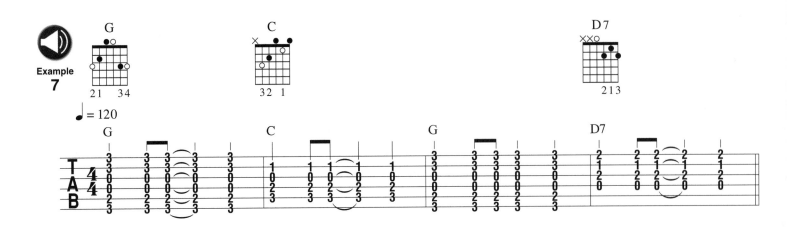

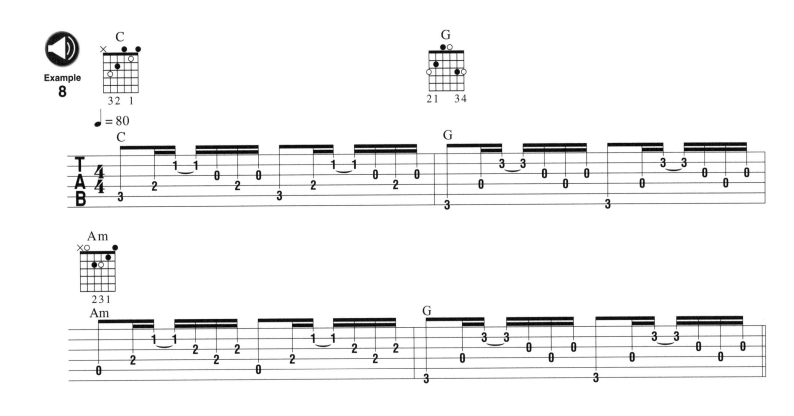

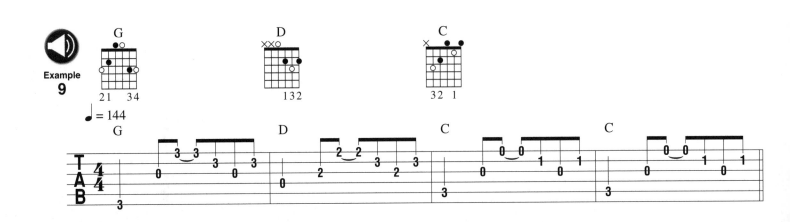

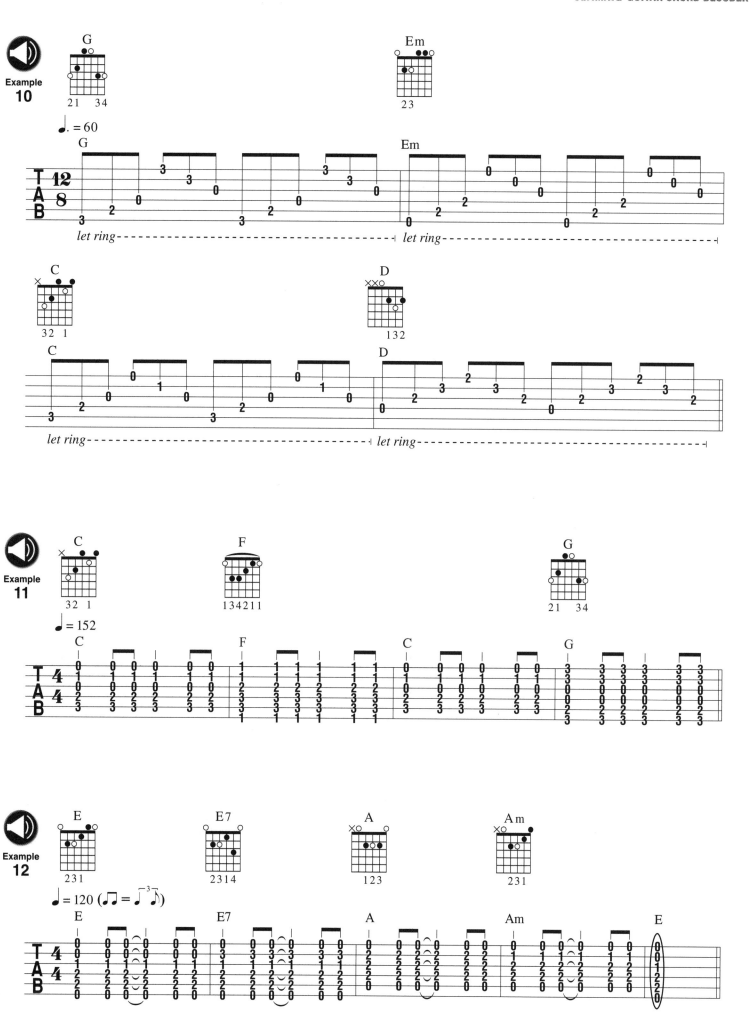

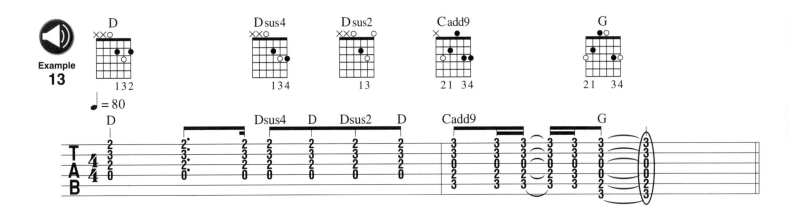

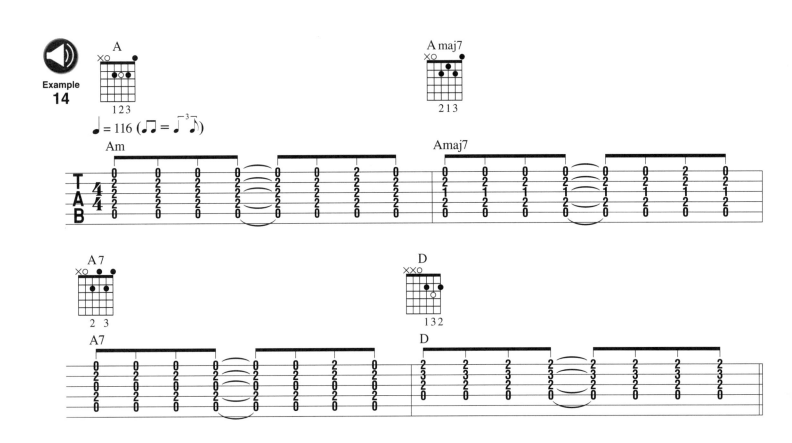

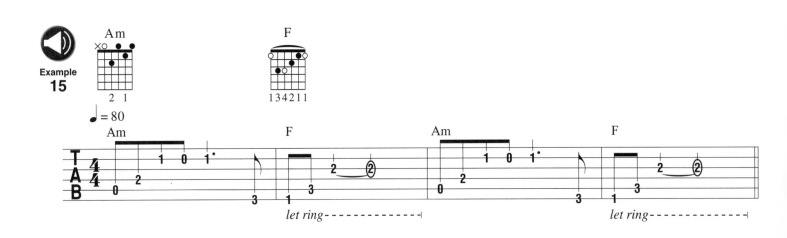

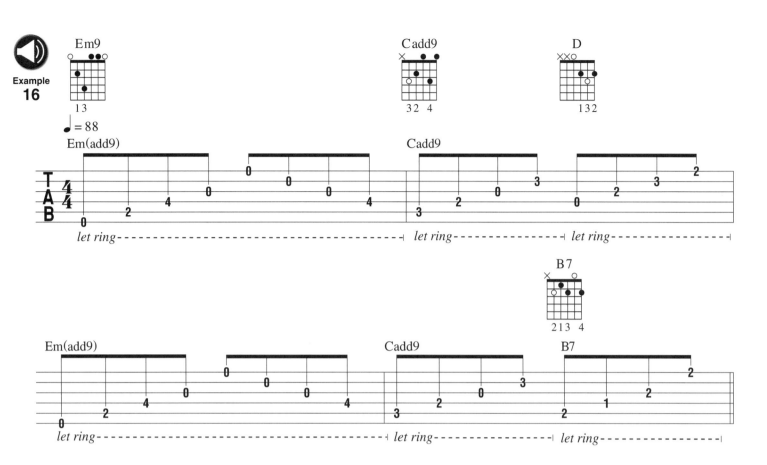

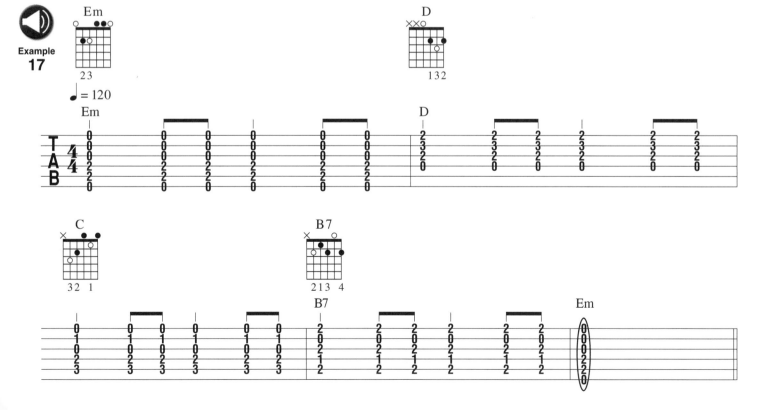

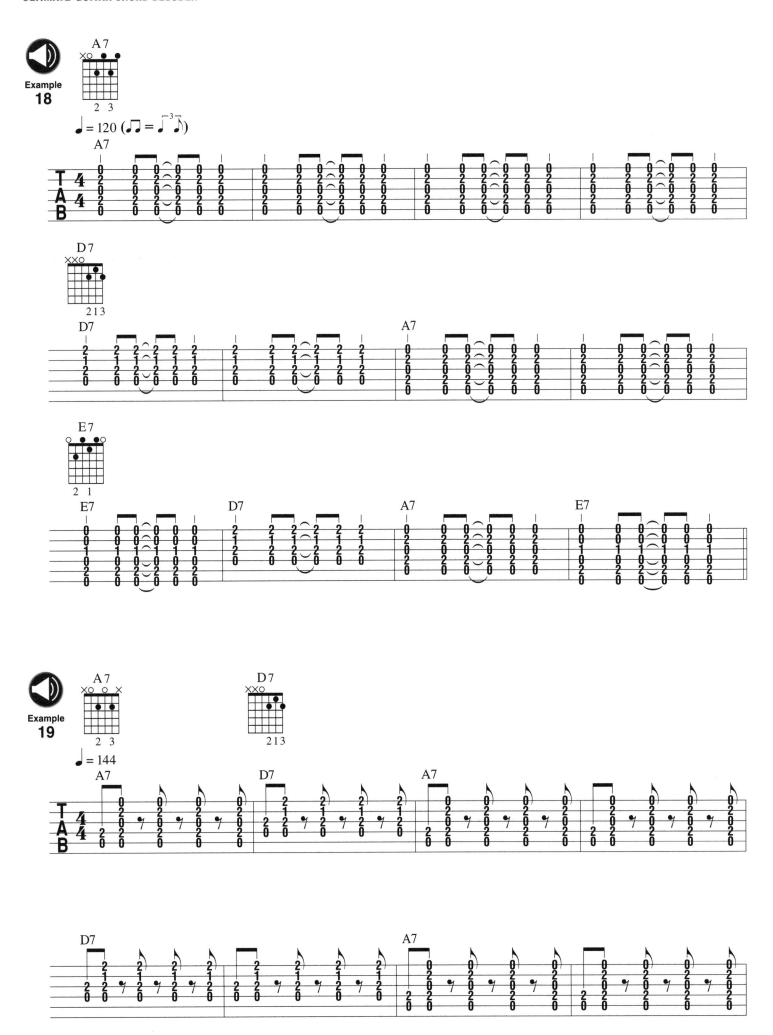

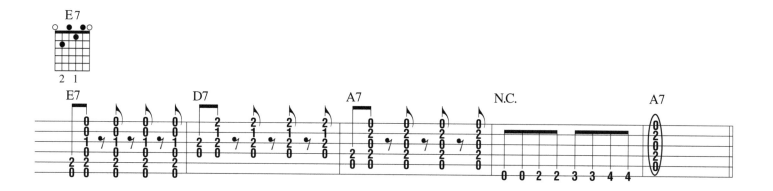

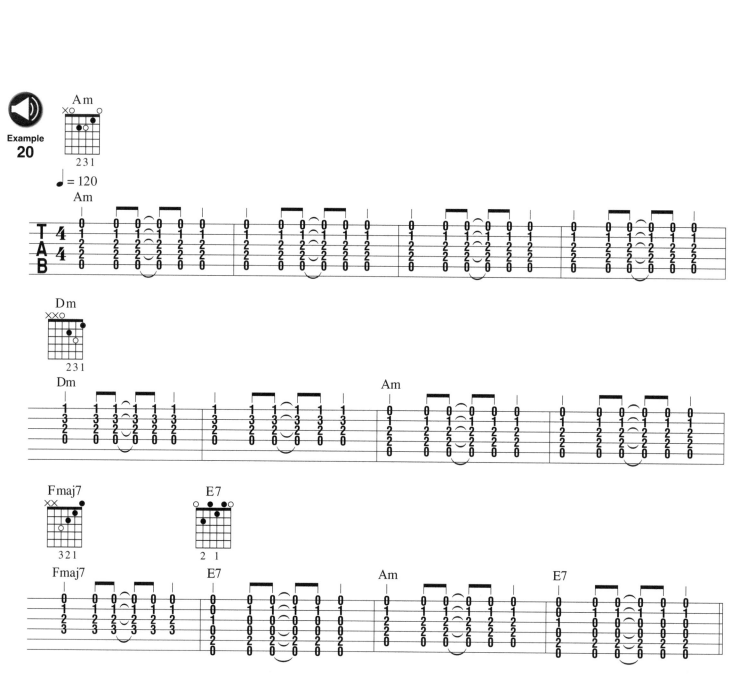

MOVEABLE CHORDS

Moveable chords are derived from open chords. To experience this firsthand, play an open A chord, but re-finger it with 2, 3, and 4 (as opposed to the indicated 1, 2, and 3). Now, move that chord up one fret and play it. Every note moved has formly except the open strings, which remained in their original location. This is why we need to use barres. Take your first finger and flatten it across the top 5 strings at the first fret. The barre simulates the nut and replaces what were the open string notes. The shape and quality of the chord is maintained, it is simply moved to a different location. The root has changed from the open fifth string to the fifth string. First fret, which is B♭. You now have a B♭ chord!

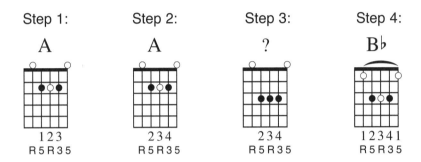

In this book, each chord shape is displayed in TAB starting from the lowest point possible on the guitar neck and then moving up chromatically fret-by-fret. Even though all of the keys are presented in TAB, it's well worth trying to memorize the names of the notes on the lower guitar strings so you can transpose any moveable chord shape without having to refer back to the TAB.

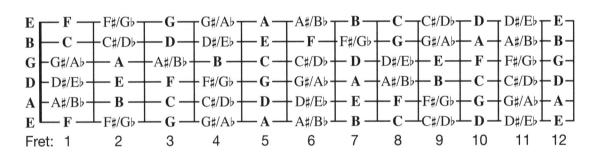

If the chord's root is on the sixth string, use this guide to transpose the shape. Eventually, try to memorize these notes.

E	F	F♯/G♭	G	G♯/A♭	A	A♯/B♭	B	C	C♯/D♭	D	D♯/E♭	E
Fret: 1	2	3	4	5	6	7	8	9	10	11	12	

If the chord's root is on the fifth string, use this guide to transpose. Eventually, try to memorize these notes.

A	A♯/B♭	B	C	C♯/D♭	D	D♯/E♭	E	F	F♯/G♭	G	G♯/A♭	A
Fret: 1	2	3	4	5	6	7	8	9	10	11	12	

If the chord's root is on the fourth string, use this guide to transpose. Eventually, try to memorize these notes.

D	D♯/E♭	E	F	F♯/G♭	G	G♯/A♭	A	A♯/B♭	B	C	C♯/D♭	D
Fret: 1	2	3	4	5	6	7	8	9	10	11	12	

Power Chords

Power chords are the backbone of all things rock or metal. The great thing about them is that since they only contain two notes—the root and the 5th—they are easy to play. Most power chord-based songs just take that one shape and move it through a simple progression. How else can the bad boys of rock run and jump around onstage all night and not make mistakes all over the place?

The most common power chord is the two-string shape.

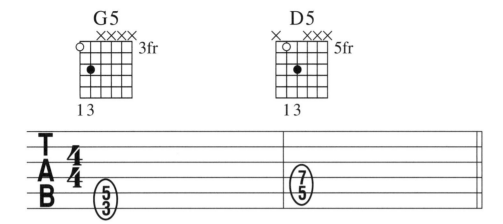

For added weight, the three-string power chord shape can also be used. If the chord has its root on strings 6 or 5, you can use a middle-finger barre to catch the extra note.

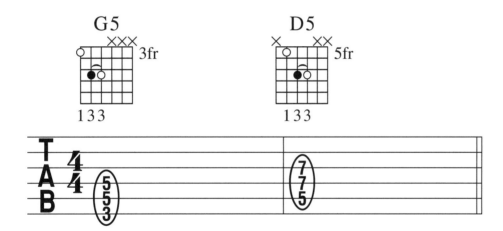

Also included are two variations on moveable power chords; the 6 and the ♭5 chord. Technically speaking, the 6 chords shown here aren't true 6 chords because there is no 3rd present. This is also the case with some of the 6 and 7 open position power chords we looked at in the "Open Position Essential Chords" chapter. But in its most typical context, as a blues chord, it implies the tonality of a 6 chord. Listen to some of the examples on the CD to hear this.

5th Power Chords

Sixth string Root

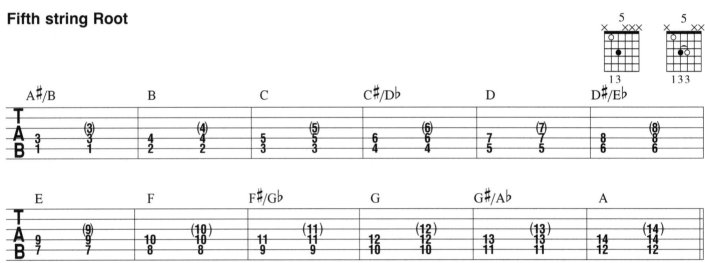

Fifth string Root

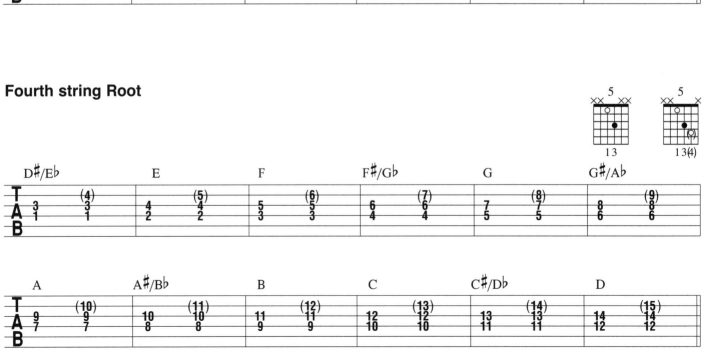

Fourth string Root

6th Power Chords

Sixth string Root

*6

F6	F#/Gb6	G6	G#/Ab6	A6	A#/Bb6

```
T
A
B  5      6      7      8      9      10
   1      2      3      4      5      6
```

B6	C6	C#/Db6	D6	D#/Eb6	E6

```
T
A
B  11     12     13     14     15     16
   7      8      9      10     11     12
```

Fifth string Root

6

A#/Bb6	B6	C6	C#/Db6	D6	D#/Eb6

```
T
A
B  5      6      7      8      9      10
   1      2      3      4      5      6
```

E6	F6	F#/Gb6	G6	G#/Ab6	A6

```
T
A
B  11     12     13     14     15     16
   7      8      9      10     11     12
```

Fourth string Root

6

D#/Eb6	E6	F6	F#/Gb6	G6	G#/Ab6

```
T
A
B  5      6      7      8      9      10
   1      2      3      4      5      6
```

A6	A#/Bb6	B6	C6	C#/Db6	D6

```
T
A
B  11     12     13     14     15     16
   7      8      9      10     11     12
```

♭5th Power Chords

Sixth string Root

1 2(3)

F(♭5)	F♯/G♭(♭5)	G(♭)	G♯/A♭(5)	A(♭5)	A♯/B♭(♭5)
(3) 2 1	(4) 3 2	(5) 4 3	(6) 5 4	(7) 6 5	(8) 7 6

B(♭5)	C(♭5)	C♯/D♭(♭5)	D(♭5)	D♯/E♭(♭5)	E(♭5)
(9) 8 7	(10) 9 8	(11) 10 9	(12) 11 10	(13) 12 11	(14) 13 12

Fifth string Root

1 2(3)

A♯/B♭(♭5)	B(♭5)	C(♭5)	C♯/D♭(♭5)	D(♭5)	D♯/E♭(♭5)
(3) 2 1	(4) 3 2	(5) 4 3	(6) 5 4	(7) 6 5	(8) 7 6

E(♭5)	F(♭5)	F♯/G♭(♭5)	G(♭5)	G♯/A♭(♭5)	A(♭)
(9) 8 7	(10) 9 8	(11) 10 9	(12) 11 10	(13) 12 11	(14) 13 12

Fourth string Root

1 2(4)

D♯/E♭(♭5)	E(♭5)	F(♭5)	F♯/G♭(♭5)	G(♭5)	G♯/A♭(♭5)
(4) 2 1	(5) 3 2	(6) 4 3	(7) 5 4	(8) 6 5	(9) 7 6

A(♭5)	A♯/B♭(♭5)	B(♭5)	C(♭5)	C♯/D♭(♭5)	D(♭5)
(10) 8 7	(11) 9 8	(12) 10 9	(13) 11 10	(14) 12 11	(15) 13 12

Music Examples

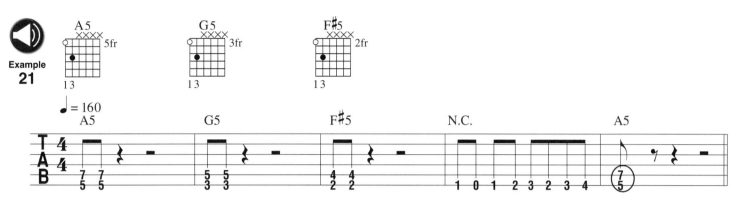

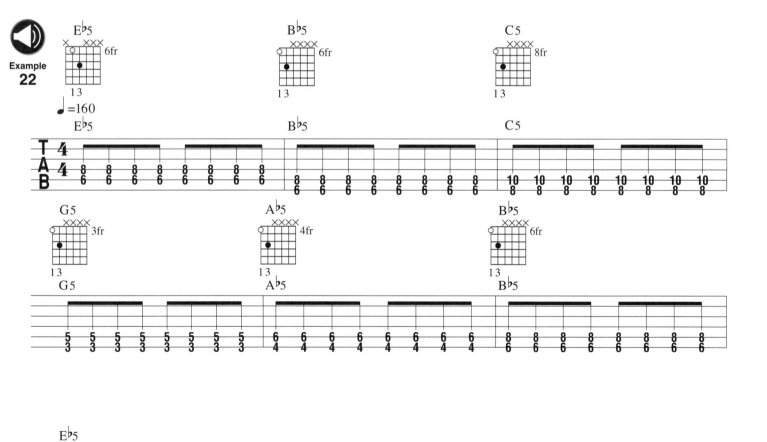

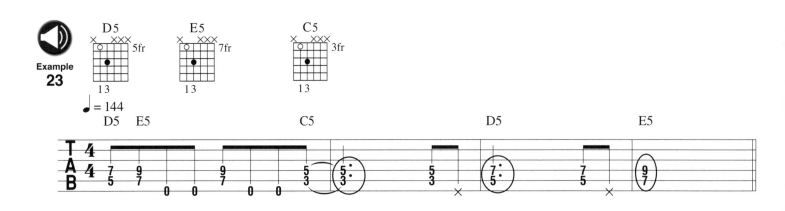

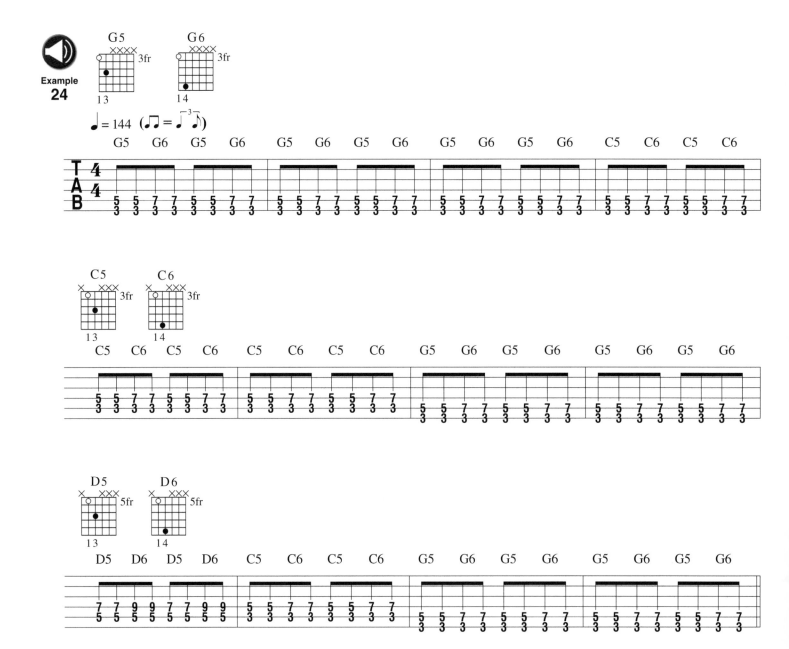

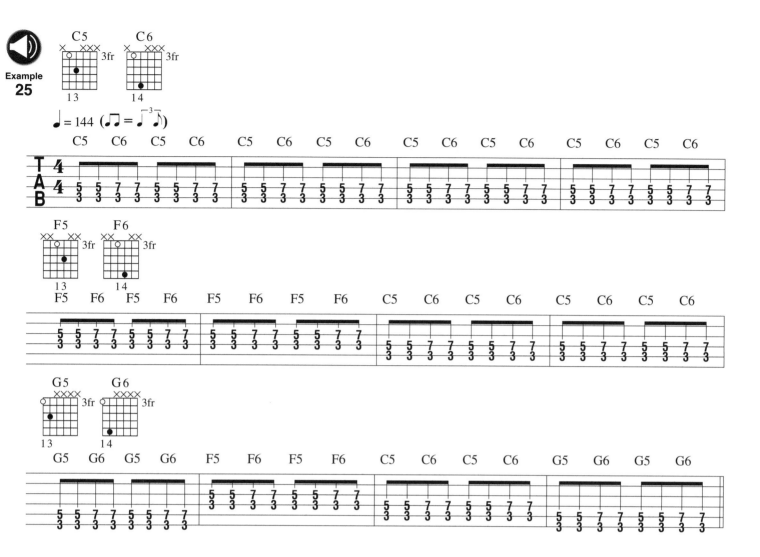

Triads

The most essential moveable chord shapes are the triad barre chords; particularly the major and minor shapes. In learning just these two chord types, you'll be able to play virtually any rock or pop song.

Technically speaking, *triads* are three note chords derived from the notes of a scale. (If you want to learn more about scales, a good source is the companion book, *The Ultimate-Guitar Scale Decoder.*) Every scale has a root note, which is the key center of the scale, as well as some kind of 3rd, 5th, and 7th. It is the 3rd and 7th that define a chord's quality.

If we take the 1st, 3rd, and 5th note or degree of any major scale and play those three notes simultaneously, we get a major triad.

In the key of C, a C major triad is spelled:

C	E	G
1	3	5

C	D	E	F	G	A	B	C
1	2	3	4	5	6	7	8

Other triads can be created by changing some notes of the major triad formula. A minor triad is created by flatting (or lowering) the 3rd degree of the major chord.

Again using C major as a reference, a C minor triad is spelled:

C	E♭	G
1	♭3	5

If you know the minor scales, you'll also realize that a minor triad consists of the root, ♭3rd, and 5th, which comes directly from the scale. That's another way of looking at it.

Common embellishments—or replacements even—for major and minor triads are sus chords, which replace a chord's 3rd with either a 4th (sus4) or a 2nd (sus2). These chords are used to create excitement and momentum.

Two other fundamental triads are the augmented and diminished triads. An augmented triad is created by sharping (or raising) the 5th degree of the major chord.

A C augmented triad is spelled:

C	E	G♯
1	3	♯5

A diminished triad is created by flatting (or lowering) the 3rd and 5th degrees of the major chord.

A C diminished triad is spelled:

C	E♭	G♭
1	♭3	♭5

You might wonder why, if triads only contain three notes, there are sometimes up to six notes played in the barre chord triad shapes shown. In these cases, some of the notes are doubled or tripled. The sixth string root barre chord shapes for the major and minor triads have three roots in the voicing on the low E, D, and high E strings respectively.

In the final chapter, "Triads and Inversions," we'll explore triad shapes with only three notes.

Major

Sixth string Root

134211

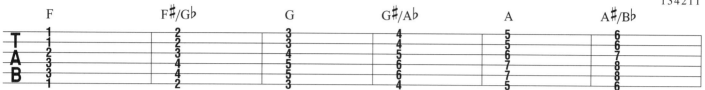

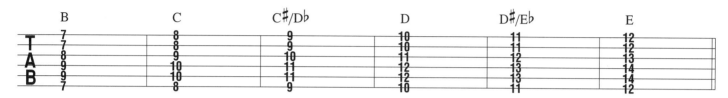

Fifth string Root

12341

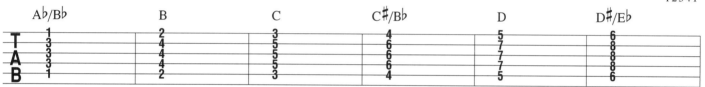

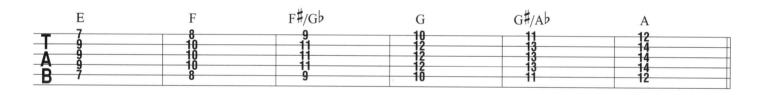

Minor

Sixth string Root

134111

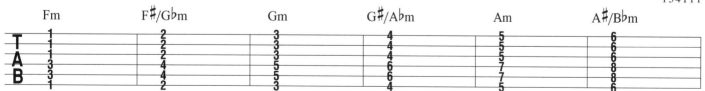

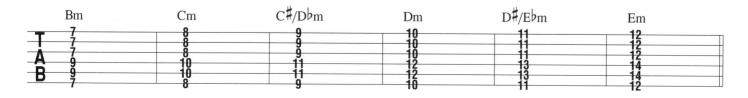

Fifth string Root

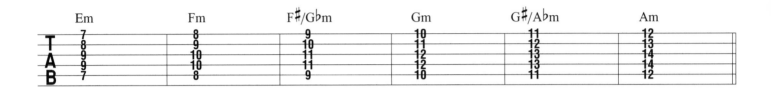

Sus4

Sixth string Root

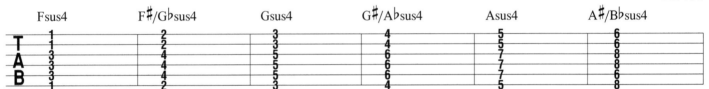

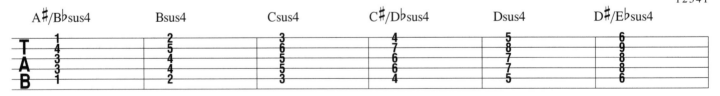

Fifth string Root

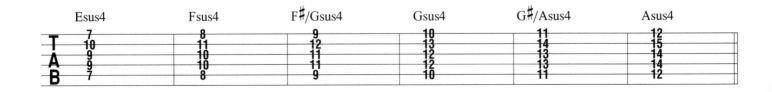

Sus2

Fifth string Root Page

13411

A#/Bbsus2   Bsus2   Csus2   C#/Dbsus2   Dsus2   D#/Ebsus2

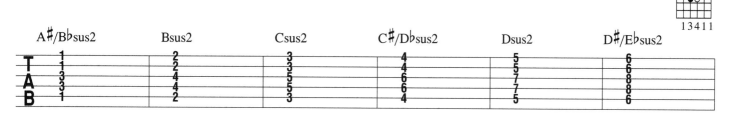

Esus2   Fsus2   F#/Gbsus2   Gsus2   G#/Absus2   Asus2

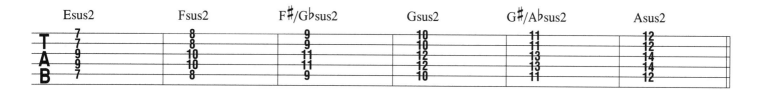

Aug

Sixth string Root

43211

G#/Ab+   A+   A#/Bb+   B+   C+   C#/Db+

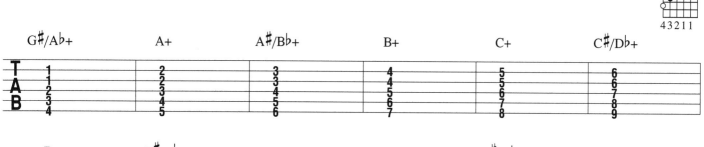

D+   D#/Eb+   E+   F+   F#/Gb+   G+

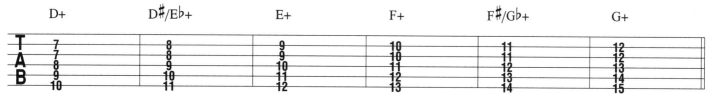

Fifth string Root

3211

C+   C#/Db+   D+   D#/Eb+   E+   F+

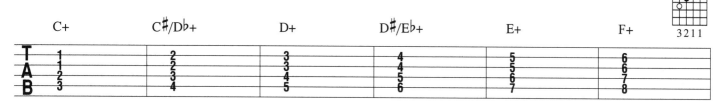

F#/Gb+   G+   G#/Ab+   A+   A#/Bb+   B+

Dim

Sixth string Root

1 2 3 1

	Fdim	F#/Gbdim	Gdim	G#/Abdim	Adim	A#/Bbdim
T	1	2	3	4	5	6
A	3	4	5	6	7	8
B	2	3	4	5	6	7
	1	2	3	4	5	6

	Bdim	Cdim	C#/Bbdim	Ddim	D#/Ebdim	Edim
T	7	8	9	10	11	12
A	9	10	11	12	13	14
B	8	9	10	11	12	13
	7	8	9	10	11	12

Fifth string Root

1 2 4 3

	A#/Bbdim	Bdim	Cdim	C#/Dbdim	Ddim	D#/Ebdim
T	2	3	4	5	6	7
A	3	4	5	6	7	8
	2	3	4	5	6	7
B	1	2	3	4	5	6

	Edim	Fdim	F#/Gbdim	Gdim	G#/Abdim	Adim
T	8	9	10	11	12	13
A	9	10	11	12	13	14
	8	9	10	11	12	13
B	7	8	9	10	11	12

Music Examples

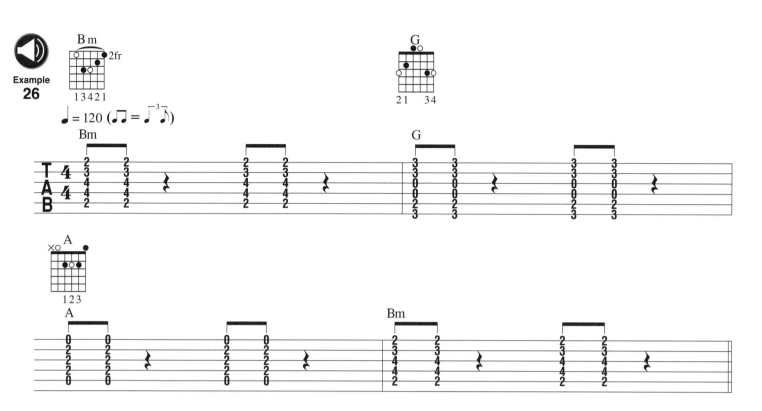

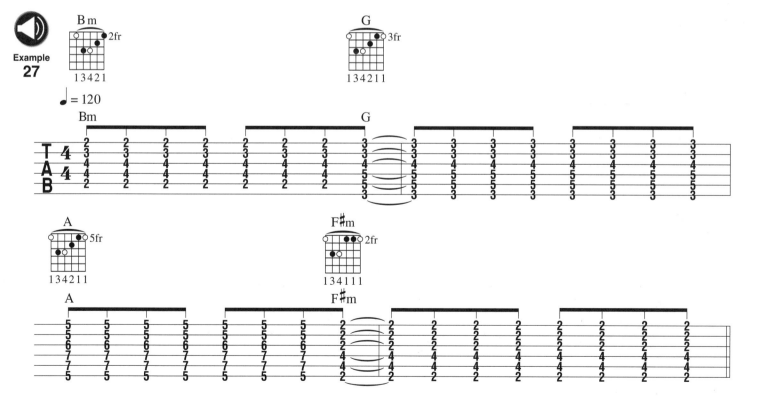

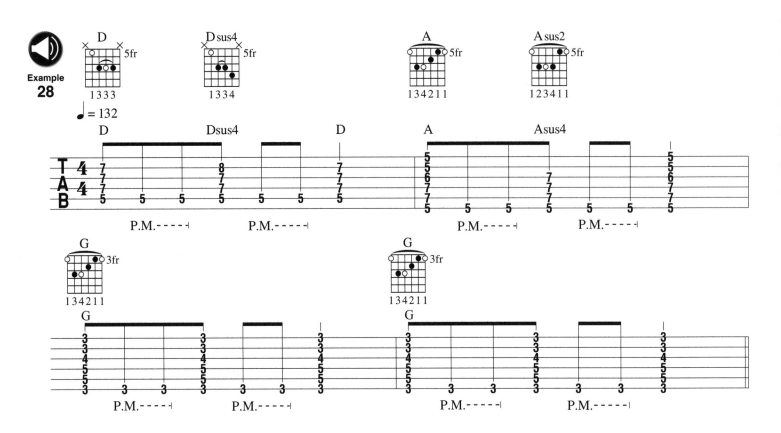

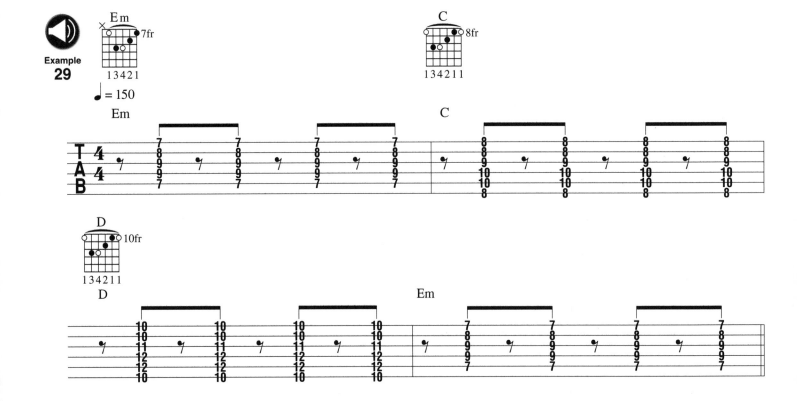

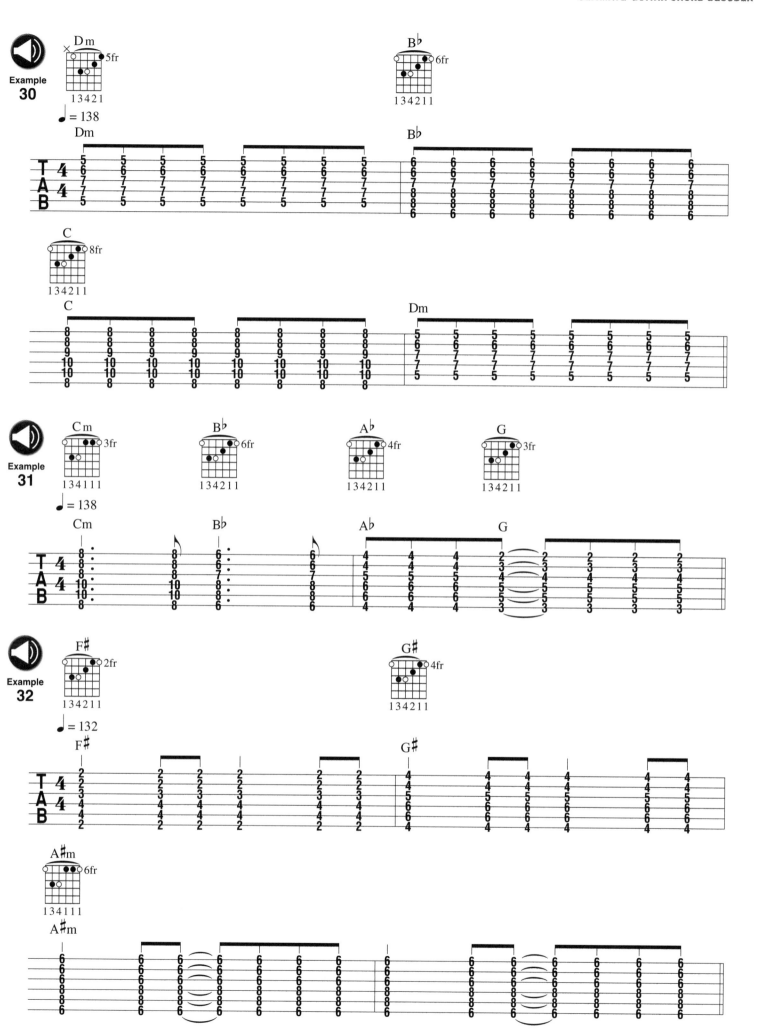

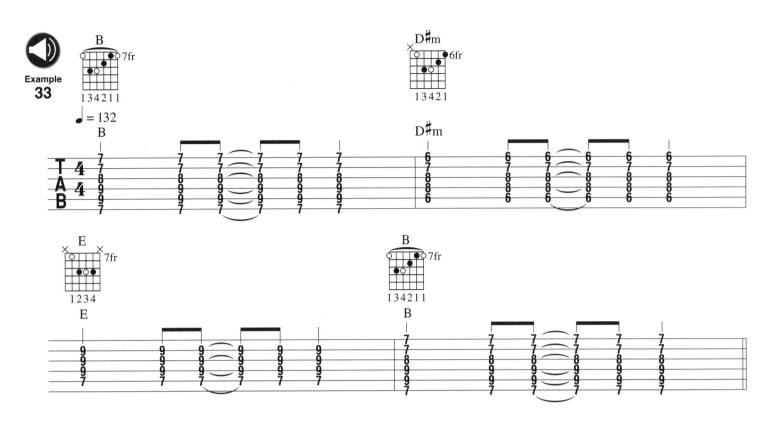

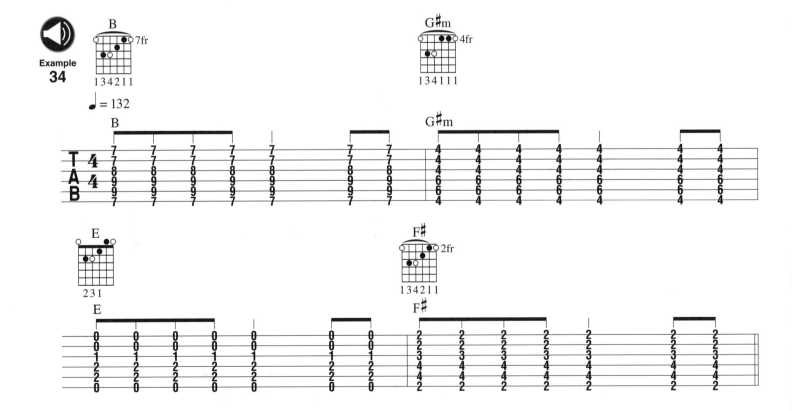

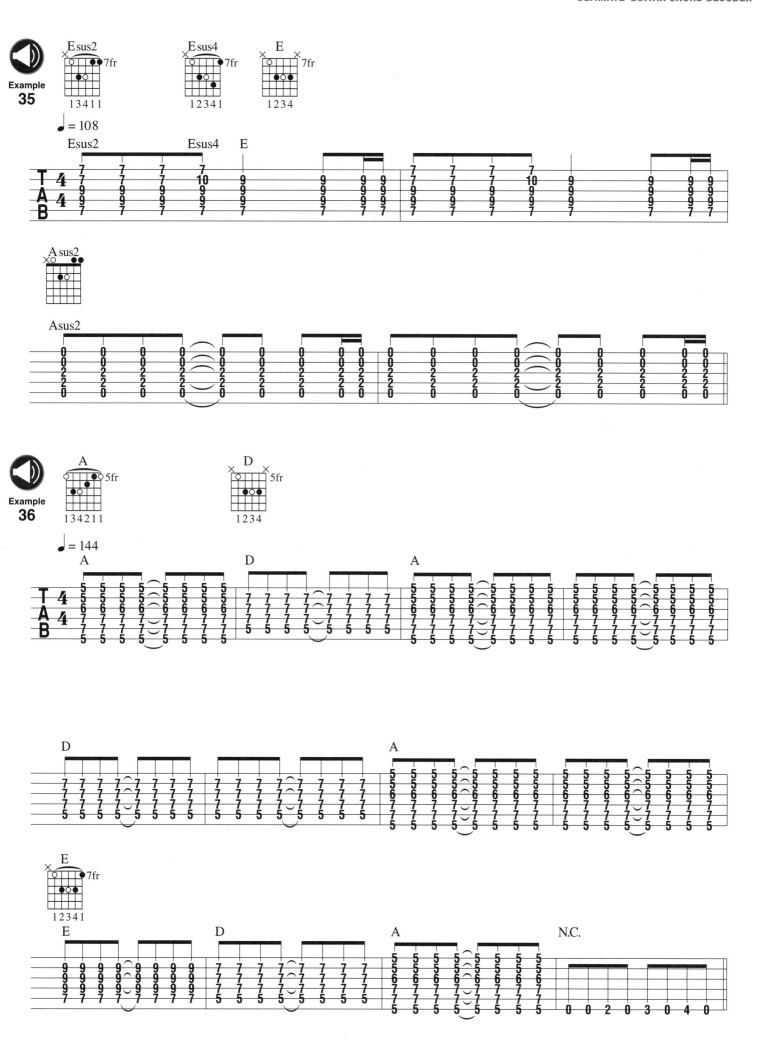

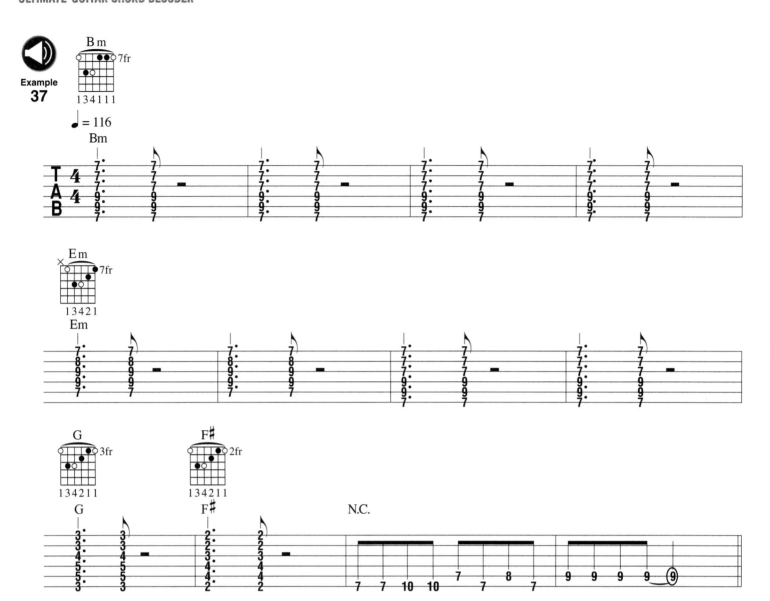

BEYOND TRIADS

Triads with Added Notes

For color, notes like the 6th, 9th, or both, are commonly added to basic triads. If you're not sure what a 9th is, refer to the upcoming chapter, "Chords with Extensions and/or Alterations" on page 42.

For example, a C6 is spelled:

C		E		G	A		
1		3		5	6		
C	D	E	F	G	A	B	C
1	2	3	4	5	6	7	8

On page 91 is a chord formula chart for you to refer to.

Seventh Chords

Seventh chords are triads with the 7th degree of the scale added. There are five basic types of seventh chords: major 7, dominant 7, minor 7 (or m/maj7, a variation), minor 7♭5, and diminished 7. All are derived from one of the basic triads we have looked at.

1) A major 7 chord consists of the root (first note), 3rd, 5th, and 7th degrees of a major scale.

A Cmaj7 is spelled:

C		E		G		B	
1		3		5		7	
C	D	E	F	G	A	B	C
1	2	3	4	5	6	7	8

2) A dominant 7 chord consists of the root (first note), 3rd, 5th, and ♭7th degrees of a major scale.

A C7 is spelled:

C		E		G		B♭
1		3		5		♭7

3) A minor 7 chord consists of the root (first note), ♭3rd, 5th, and ♭7th degrees of a major scale.

A Cmin7 is spelled:

C		E♭		G		B♭
1		♭3		5		♭7

4) A m/maj7 chord is a min7 chord with a major 7th, rather than a flat 7th.

A Cm/maj7 is spelled:

C	E♭	G	B
1	♭3	5	7

5) A minor 7♭5 chord consists of the root (first note), ♭3rd, ♭5th, and ♭7th degrees of a major scale.

A Cmin7♭5 is spelled:

C	E♭	G♭	B♭
1	♭3	♭5	♭7

6) A diminished 7 chord consists of the root (first note), ♭3rd, ♭5th, and ♭♭7th degrees of a major scale.

A Cdim7 is spelled:

C	E♭	G♭	B♭♭
1	♭3	♭5	♭♭7

Chords with Extensions and/or Alterations

Chords like 9th, 11th, and 13th chords take the concept of 7th chords to the next level. Typically, the 8th degree of a scale or mode is the same note as the 1st degree, just an octave higher. From that point on, the scale starts over again, just in the next higher octave. Beyond the octave, the 2nd, 4th, and 6th degrees are referred to as the 9th, 11th, and 13th. These notes function as *chord extensions* and can generally be added to any of the seventh chord types we looked at for extra color. You'll hear these types of chords quite often in jazz and much less often in rock or metal.

For example, here are the notes of the C Dorian mode shown with chord tones and extensions:

1		♭3		5		♭7		9		11		13	
C	D	E♭	F	G	A	B♭	C	D	E♭	F	G	A	B

In relation to a root, every note of a scale has a distinctive sound and function. The fundamental chord tones define a chord's tonality while the extensions serve to add color. The thing to realize is that while extensions add significant flavor to the overall sound of a chord, they don't change the basic quality of the chord. For example, a minor 11 chord is just a more colorful version of a minor 7 chord. The important thing to note is which seventh chord family the chord belongs to: major 7, dominant 7, minor 7, minor 7♭5, or diminished 7.

In the majority of cases, not all of the notes that are theoretically possible are actually played simultaneously in a chord voicing. The chord symbol Cm13 implies the presence of the fundamental chord tones plus the extensions 9, 11, and 13. Whether all, only a few, or none of the possible chord extensions are played at a given moment, it is understood that they are available options to choose from depending on the color desired.

Deciphering Chord Symbols

Complex chords are usually named in the following order: Root, quality, and uppermost extension (C13, for example). Altered notes are mentioned last (C13♭9, for example). Alterations are chromatic changes made to either chord tones or extensions (♯5 or ♭9, for example).

The system of naming chords isn't completely standardized. Therefore, you might refer to a chord one way only to see it presented differently by someone else or in another book.

Here are some of the most common chord symbols that you'll see:

CHORD TYPE	CHORD NAME
major 7	maj7, M7, 7△
7	7, dom7
minor 7	m7, min7, -7
m7♭5	ø
diminished 7	°7, dim7
augmented 7	+7, 7♯5, aug7
minor/major 7	m(maj7), -(maj7)

Note that these symbols also apply to the extended and/or altered versions of these chords. For example, Cminor 7 can be referred to as Cm7 or C-7, Cminor 9 can be referred to as Cm9 or C-9, Cminor 11 can be referred to as Cm11 or C-11, and Cminor 13 can be referred to as Cm 13 or C-13.

Add9

Sixth string Root

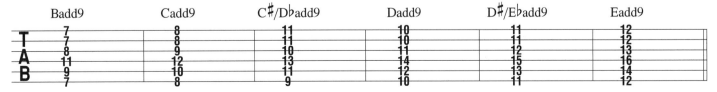

Fadd9	F♯/G♭add9	Gadd9	G♯/Aadd9	Aadd9	A♯/B♭add9

```
    1        2        3        4        5        6
T   1        2        3        4        5        6
A   2        3        4        5        6        7
    5        6        7        8        9       10
B   3        4        5        6        7        8
    1        2        3        4        5        6
```

Badd9	Cadd9	C♯/D♭add9	Dadd9	D♯/E♭add9	Eadd9

```
    7        8       11       10       11       12
T   7        8       11       10       11       12
A   8        9       10       11       12       13
   11       12       13       14       15       16
B   9       10       11       12       13       14
    7        8        9       10       11       12
```

43

Fifth string Root

12431

	A♯/B♭add9	Badd9	Cadd9	C♯/D♭add9	Dadd9	D♯/E♭add9
T	1	2	3	4	5	6
	3	4	5	6	5	8
A	5	6	7	8	9	10
	3	4	5	6	7	8
B	1	2	3	4	5	6

	Eadd9	Fadd9	F♯/G♭add9	Gadd9	G♯/A♭add9	Aadd9
T	7	8	9	10	11	12
	9	10	11	12	13	14
A	11	12	13	14	15	16
	9	10	11	12	13	14
B	7	8	9	10	11	12

Fifth string Root

3214

	C♯/D♭add9	Dadd9	D♯/E♭add9	Eadd9	Fadd9	F♯/G♭add9
T	4	5	6	7	8	9
	1	2	3	4	5	6
A	3	4	5	6	7	8
	4	5	6	7	8	9
B						

	Gadd9	G♯/A♭add9	Aadd9	A♯/B♭add9	Badd9	Cadd9
T	10	11	12	13	14	15
	7	8	9	10	11	12
A	9	10	11	12	13	14
	10	11	12	13	14	15
B						

Fourth string Root

3214

	Fadd9	F♯/G♭add9	Gadd9	G♯/A♭add9	Aadd9	A♯/B♭add9
T	3	4	5	6	7	8
	1	2	3	4	5	6
A	2	3	4	5	6	7
	3	4	5	6	7	8
B						

	Badd9	Cadd9	C♯/D♭add9	Dadd9	D♯/E♭add9	Eadd9
T	9	10	11	12	13	14
	7	8	9	10	11	12
A	8	9	10	11	12	13
	9	10	11	12	13	14
B						

madd9

Sixth string Root

134111

Fm(add9)	F#/G♭m(add9)	Gm(add9)	G#/A♭m(add9)	Am(add9)	A#/B♭m(add9)

```
T  1        2        3        4        5        6
A  1        2        3        4        5        6
   1        2        3        4        5        6
B  5        6        7        8        9        10
   3        4        5        6        7        8
   1        2        3        4        5        6
```

Bm(add9)	Cm(add9)	C#/D♭(add9)	Dm(add9)	D#/E♭(add9)	Em(add9)

```
T  7        8        9        10       11       12
A  7        8        9        10       11       12
   7        8        9        10       11       12
B  11       12       13       14       15       16
   9        10       11       12       13       14
   7        8        9        10       11       12
```

Fifth string Root

13421

A#/B♭m(add9)	Bm(add9)	Cm(add9)	C#/D♭m(add9)	Dm(add9)	D#/E♭m(add9)

```
T  1        2        3        4        5        6
A  2        3        4        5        6        7
   5        6        7        8        9        10
   3        4        5        6        7        8
B  1        2        3        4        5        6
```

Em(add9)	Fm(add9)	F#/G♭m(add9)	Gm(add9)	G#/A♭m(add9)	Am(add9)

```
T  7        8        9        10       11       12
A  8        9        10       11       12       13
   11       12       13       14       15       16
   9        10       11       12       13       14
B  7        8        9        10       11       12
```

Fifth string Root

3214

C#/D♭m(add9)	Dm(add9)	D#/E♭m(add9)	Em(add9)	Fm(add9)	F#/G♭m(add9)

```
T  4        5        6        7        8        9
A  1        2        3        4        5        6
   2        3        4        5        6        7
B  4        5        6        7        8        9
```

Gm(add9)	G#/A♭m(add9)	Am(add9)	A#/B♭m(add9)	Bm(add9)	Cm(add9)

```
T  10       11       12       13       14       15
A  7        8        9        10       11       12
   8        9        10       11       12       13
B  10       11       12       13       14       15
```

Fourth string Root

3114

Fm(add9)	F♯/G♭m(add9)	Gm(add9)	G♯/A♭m(add9)	Am(add9)	A♯/B♭m(add9)
3	4	5	6	7	8
1	2	3	4	5	6
1	2	3	4	5	6
3	4	5	6	7	8

Bm(add9)	Cm(add9)	C♯/D♭m(add9)	Dm(add9)	D♯/E♭m(add9)	Em(add9)
9	10	11	12	13	14
7	8	9	10	11	12
7	8	9	10	11	12
9	10	11	12	13	14

6

Sixth string Root

2 143

F♯/G♭6	G6	G♯/A♭6	A6	A♯/B♭6	B6
2	3	4	5	6	7
3	4	5	6	7	8
1	2	3	4	5	6
2	3	4	5	6	7

C6	C♯/D♭6	D6	D♯/E♭6	E6	F6
8	9	10	11	12	13
9	10	11	12	13	14
7	8	9	10	11	12
8	9	10	11	12	13

Fifth string Root

2314

B6	C6	C♯/D♭6	D6	D♯/E♭6	E6
4	5	6	7	8	9
1	2	3	4	5	6
4	5	6	7	8	9
2	3	4	5	6	7

F6	F♯/G♭6	G6	G♯/A♭6	A6	A♯/B♭6
10	11	12	13	14	15
7	8	9	10	11	12
10	11	12	13	14	15
8	9	10	11	12	13

Fifth string Root

4 2 3 1

	C6	C#/Db6	D6	D#/Eb6	E6	F6
T	1	2	3	4	5	6
A	2	3	4	5	6	7
	2	3	4	5	6	7
B	3	4	5	6	7	8

	F#/Gb6	G6	G#/Ab6	A6	A#/Bb6	B6
T	7	8	9	10	11	12
A	8	9	10	11	12	13
	8	9	10	11	12	13
B	9	10	11	12	13	14

Fourth string Root

1 3 1 4

	D#/Eb6	E6	F6	F#/Gb6	G6	G#/Ab6
T	3	4	5	6	7	8
A	1	2	3	4	5	6
	3	4	5	6	7	8
B	1	2	3	4	5	6

	A6	A#/Bb6	B6	C6	C#/Db6	D6
T	9	10	11	12	13	14
A	7	8	9	10	11	12
	9	10	11	12	13	14
B	7	8	9	10	11	12

m6

Sixth string Root

2 1 3 4

	F#/Gbm6	Gm6	G#/Abm6	Am6	A#/Bbm6	Bm6
T	2	3	4	5	6	7
A	2	3	4	5	6	7
	1	2	3	4	5	6
B	2	3	4	5	6	7

	Cm6	C#/Dbm6	Dm6	D#/Ebm6	Em6	Fm6
T	8	9	10	11	12	13
A	8	9	10	11	12	13
	7	8	9	10	11	12
B	8	9	11	11	12	13

Fifth string Root

2 4 1 3

	Bm6	Cm6	C♯/D♭m6	Dm6	D♯/E♭m6	Em6
T	3	4	5	6	7	8
	1	2	3	4	5	6
A	4	5	6	7	8	9
B	2	3	4	5	6	7

	Fm6	F♯/G♭m6	Gm6	G♯/A♭m6	Am6	A♯/B♭m6
T	9	10	11	12	13	14
	7	8	9	10	11	12
A	10	11	12	13	14	15
B	8	9	10	11	12	13

Fifth string Root

3 1 2 1

	Cm6	C♯/D♭m6	Dm6	D♯/E♭m6	Em6	Fm6
T	1	2	3	4	5	0
	2	3	4	5	6	7
A	1	2	3	4	5	6
B	3	4	5	6	7	8

	F♯/G♭m6	Gm6	G♯/A♭m6	Am6	A♯/B♭m6	Bm6
T	7	10	9	10	11	12
	8	9	10	11	12	13
A	7	8	9	10	11	12
B	9	10	11	12	13	14

Fourth string Root

1 3 1 2

	D♯/E♭m6	Em6	Fm6	F♯/G♭m6	Gm6	G♯/A♭m6
T	2	3	4	5	6	7
	1	2	3	4	5	6
A	3	4	5	6	7	8
	1	2	3	4	5	6
B						

	Am6	A♯/B♭m6	Bm6	Cm6	C♯/D♭m6	Dm6
T	8	9	10	11	12	13
	7	8	9	10	11	12
A	9	10	11	12	13	14
	7	8	9	10	11	12
B						

6/9

Sixth string Root

211134

F#/Gb6/9	G6/9	G#/Ab6/9	A6/9	A#/Bb6/9	B6/9
2 2 1 1 2	3 3 2 2 3	4 4 3 3 4	5 5 4 4 5	6 6 5 5 6	7 7 6 6 7

C6/9	C#/Db6/9	D6/9	D#/Eb6/9	E6/9	F6/9
8 8 7 7 8	9 9 8 8 9	10 10 9 9 10	11 11 10 10 11	12 12 11 11 12	13 13 12 12 13

Fifth string Root

21134

B6/9	C6/9	C#/Db6/9	D6/9	D#/Eb6/9	E6/9
2 2 1 1 2	3 3 2 2 3	4 4 3 3 4	5 5 4 4 5	6 6 5 5 6	7 7 6 6 7

F6/9	F#/Gb6/9	G6/9	G#/Ab6/9	A6/9	A#/Bb6/9
8 8 7 7 8	9 9 8 8 9	10 10 9 9 10	11 11 10 10 11	12 12 11 11 12	13 13 12 12 13

m6/9

Sixth string Root

4123

Gm6/9	G#/Abm6/9	Am6/9	A#/Bbm6/9	Bm6/9	Cm6/9
2 2 1 3	3 3 2 4	4 4 3 5	5 5 4 6	6 6 5 7	7 7 6 8

C#/Dbm6/9	Dm6/9	D#/Ebm6/9	Em6/9	Fm6/9	F#/Gbm6/9
8 8 7 9	9 9 8 10	10 10 9 11	11 11 10 12	12 12 11 13	13 13 12 14

Fifth string Root

3 1 2 4

	Cm6/9	C#/Dbm6/9	Dm6/9	D#/Ebm6/9	Em6/9	Fm6/9
	3	4	5	6	7	8
	2	3	4	5	6	7
	1	2	3	4	5	6
	3	4	5	6	7	8

	F#/Gbm6/9	Gm6/9	G#/Abm6/9	Am6/9	A#/Bbm6/9	Bm6/9
	9	10	11	12	13	14
	8	9	10	11	12	13
	7	8	9	10	11	12
	9	10	11	12	13	14

Major Chords

Major 7

Sixth string Root

1 3 4 2

	Fmaj7	F#/Gbmaj7	Gmaj7	G#/Abmaj7	Amaj7	A#/Bbmaj7
	1	2	3	4	5	6
	2	3	4	5	6	7
	2	3	4	5	6	7
	1	2	3	4	5	6

	Bmaj7	Cmaj7	C#/Dbmaj7	Dmaj7	D#/Ebmaj7	Emaj7
	7	8	9	10	11	12
	8	9	10	11	12	13
	8	9	10	11	12	13
	7	8	9	10	11	12

Fifth string Root

1 3 2 4 1

	A#/Bbmaj7	Bmaj7	Cmaj7	C#/Dbmaj7	Dmaj7	D#/Ebmaj7
	1	2	3	4	5	6
	3	4	5	6	7	8
	2	3	4	5	6	7
	3	4	5	6	7	8
	1	2	3	4	5	6

	Emaj7	Fmaj7	F#/Gbmaj7	Gmaj7	G#/Abmaj7	Amaj7
	7	8	9	10	11	12
	9	10	11	12	13	14
	8	9	10	11	12	13
	9	10	11	12	13	14
	7	8	9	10	11	12

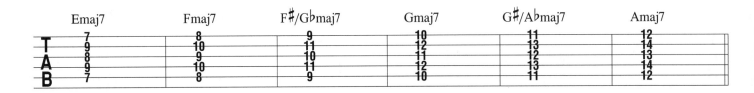

Fourth string Root

1 3 3 3

D#/Ebmaj7	Emaj7	Fmaj7	F#/Gbmaj7	Gmaj7	G#/Abmaj7
3	4	5	6	7	8
3	4	5	6	7	8
3	4	5	6	7	8
1	2	3	4	5	6

Amaj7	A#/Bbmaj7	Bmaj7	Cmaj7	C#/Dbmaj7	Dmaj7
9	10	11	12	13	14
9	10	11	12	13	14
9	10	11	12	13	14
7	8	9	10	11	12

4 3 2 1

F#/Gbmaj7	Gmaj7	G#/Abmaj7	Amaj7	A#/Bbmaj7	Bmaj7
1	2	3	4	5	6
2	3	4	5	6	7
3	4	5	6	7	8
4	5	6	7	8	9

Cmaj7	C#/Dbmaj7	Dmaj7	D#/Ebmaj7	Emaj7	Fmaj7
7	8	9	10	11	12
8	9	10	11	12	13
9	10	11	12	13	14
10	11	12	13	14	15

Maj7#11

Sixth string Root

2 3 4 1

F#/Gbmaj7#11	Gmaj7#11	G#/Abmaj7#11	Amaj7#11	A#/Bbmaj7#11	Bmaj7#11
1	2	3	4	5	6
3	4	5	6	7	8
3	4	5	6	7	8
2	3	4	5	6	7

Cmaj7#11	C#/Dbmaj7#11	Dmaj7#11	D#/Ebmaj7#11	Emaj7#11	Fmaj7#11
7	8	9	10	11	12
9	10	11	12	13	14
9	10	11	12	13	14
8	9	10	11	12	13

Fifth string Root

A#/Bbmaj7#11	Bmaj7#11	Cmaj7#11	C#/Dbmaj7#11	Dmaj7#11	D#/Ebmaj7#11
3	4	5	6	7	8
2	3	4	5	6	7
2	3	4	5	6	7
1	2	3	4	5	6

Emaj7#11	Fmaj7#11	F#/Gbmaj7#11	Gmaj7#11	G#/Abmaj7#11	Amaj7#11
9	10	11	12	13	14
8	9	10	11	12	13
8	9	10	11	12	13
7	8	9	10	11	12

Maj9

Sixth string Root

F#/Gbmaj9	Gmaj9	G#/Abmaj9	Amaj9	A#/Bbmaj9	Bmaj9
2	3	4	5	6	7
1	2	3	4	5	6
3	4	5	6	7	8
1	2	3	4	5	6
2	3	4	5	6	7

Cmaj9	C#/Dbmaj9	Dmaj9	D#/Ebmaj9	Emaj9	Fmaj9
8	9	10	11	12	13
7	8	9	10	11	12
9	10	11	12	13	14
7	8	9	10	11	12
8	9	10	11	12	13

Fifth string Root

Bmaj9	Cmaj9	C#/Dbmaj9	Dmaj9	D#/Ebmaj9	Emaj9
2	3	4	5	6	7
3	4	5	7	6	8
1	2	3	4	5	6
2	3	4	5	6	7

Fmaj9	F#/Gbmaj9	Gmaj9	G#/Abmaj9	Amaj9	A#/Bbmaj9
8	9	10	11	12	13
9	10	11	12	13	14
7	8	9	10	11	12
8	9	10	11	12	13

Major 9#11

Sixth string Root

21311

| F#/Gbmaj9#11 | Gmaj9#11 | G#/Abmaj9#11 | Amaj9#11 | A#/Bbmaj9#11 | Bmaj9#11 |

```
T  1      2      3      4      5      6
A  3      5      6      7      8      9
B  1      2      3      4      5      6
   3      4      5      6      7      8
```

| Cmaj9#11 | C#/Dbmaj9#11 | Dmaj9#11 | D#/Ebmaj9#11 | Emaj9#11 | Fmaj9#11 |

```
T  7       8        9        10       11       12
A  7       8        9        10       11       12
   9       10       11       12       13       14
B  8       9        10       11       12       13
```

Fifth string Root

21431

| Bmaj9#11 | Cmaj9#11 | C#/Dbmaj9#11 | Dmaj9#11 | D#/Ebmaj9#11 | Emaj9#11 |

```
T  1       2        3        4        5        6
A  2       3        4        5        6        7
   3       4        5        6        7        8
B  1       2        3        4        5        6
   2       3        4        5        6        7
```

| Fmaj9#11 | F#/Gbmaj9#11 | Gmaj9#11 | G#/Abmaj9#11 | Amaj9#11 | A#/Bbmaj9#11 |

```
T  7       8        9        10       11       12
A  8       9        10       11       12       13
   9       10       11       12       13       14
B  7       8        9        10       11       12
   8       9        10       11       12       13
```

Major 13

Sixth string Root

1 234

| Fmaj13 | F#/Gbmaj13 | Gmaj13 | G#/Abmaj13 | Amaj13 | A#/Bbmaj13 |

```
T  3      4      5      6      7      8
   2      3      4      5      6      7
A  2      3      4      5      6      7
B
   1      2      3      4      5      6
```

| Bmaj13 | Cmaj13 | C#/Dbmaj13 | Dmaj13 | D#/Ebmaj13 | Emaj13 |

```
T  9      10      11      12      13      14
   8      9       10      11      12      13
A  8      9       10      11      12      13
B
   7      8       9       10      11      12
```

Fifth string Root

1 2 3 4

A#/Bbmaj13	Bmaj13	Cmaj13	C#/Dbmaj13	Dmaj13	D#/Ebmaj13
3	4	5	6	7	8
3	4	5	6	7	8
2	3	4	5	6	7
1	2	3	4	5	6

Emaj13	Fmaj13	F#/Gbmaj13	Gmaj13	G#/Abmaj13	Amaj13
9	10	11	12	13	14
9	10	11	12	13	14
8	9	10	11	12	13
7	8	9	10	11	12

Maj7#5

Sixth string Root

1 2 3 4

Fmaj7#5	F#/Gbmaj7#5	Gmaj7#5	G#/Abmaj7#5	Amaj7#5	A#/Bbmaj7#5
2	3	4	5	6	7
2	3	4	5	6	7
2	3	4	5	6	7
1	2	3	4	5	6

Bmaj7#5	Cmaj7#5	C#/Dbmaj7#5	Dmaj7#5	D#/Ebmaj7#5	Emaj7#5
8	9	10	11	12	13
8	9	10	11	12	13
8	9	10	11	12	13
7	8	9	10	11	12

Fifth string Root

1 4 2 3

A#/Bbmaj7#5	Bmaj7#5	Cmaj7#5	C#/Dbmaj7#5	Dmaj7#5	D#/Ebmaj7#5
3	4	5	6	7	8
2	3	4	5	6	7
4	5	6	7	8	9
1	2	3	4	5	6

Emaj7#5	Fmaj7#5	F#/Gbmaj7#5	Gmaj7#5	G#/Abmaj7#5	Amaj7#5
9	10	11	12	13	14
8	9	10	11	12	13
10	11	12	13	14	15
7	8	9	10	11	12

Fifth string Root

A#/B♭maj7#5	Bmaj7#5	Cmaj7#5	C#/D♭maj7#5	Dmaj7#5	D#/E♭maj7#5
2	3	4	5	6	7
3	4	5	6	7	8
2	3	4	5	6	7
1	2	3	4	5	6

Emaj7#5	Fmaj7#5	F#/D♭maj7#5	Gmaj7#5	G#/A♭maj7#5	Amaj7#5
8	9	10	11	12	13
9	10	11	12	13	14
8	9	10	11	12	13
7	8	9	10	11	12

Fourth string Root

F#/G♭maj7#5	Gmaj7#5	G#/A♭maj7#5	Amaj7#5	A#/B♭maj7#5	Bmaj7#5
1	2	3	4	5	6
3	4	5	6	7	8
3	4	5	6	7	8
4	5	6	7	8	9

Cmaj7#5	C#/D♭maj7#5	Dmaj7#5	D#/E♭maj7#5	Emaj7#5	Fmaj7#5
7	8	9	10	11	12
9	10	11	12	13	14
9	10	11	12	13	14
10	11	12	13	14	15

Dominant Chords

7

Sixth string Root

F7	F#/G♭7	G7	G#/A♭7	A7	A#/B♭7
1	2	3	4	5	6
1	2	3	4	5	6
2	3	4	5	6	7
1	2	3	4	5	6
3	4	5	6	7	8
1	2	3	4	5	6

B7	C7	C#7/D♭7	D7	D#/E♭7	E7
7	8	9	10	11	12
7	8	9	10	11	12
8	9	10	11	12	13
7	8	9	10	11	12
9	10	11	12	13	14
7	8	9	10	11	12

Fifth string Root

13141

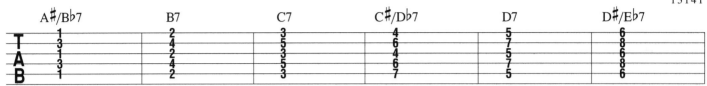

Fifth string Root

3241

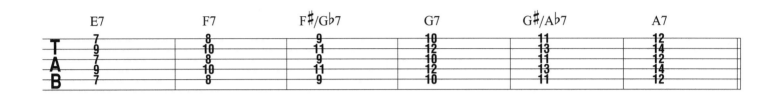

Fourth string Root

1324

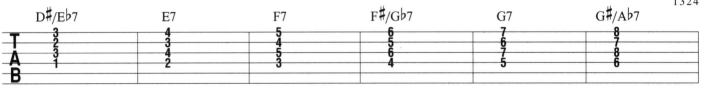

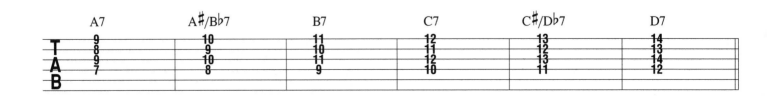

7sus4

Sixth string Root

131411

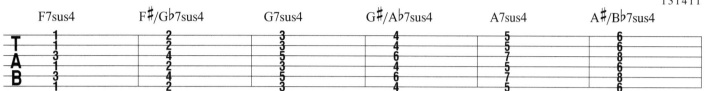

F7sus4	F#/Gb7sus4	G7sus4	G#/Ab7sus4	A7sus4	A#/Bb7sus4
1	2	3	4	5	6
1	2	3	4	5	6
3	4	5	6	7	8
3	4	5	6	7	8
1	2	3	4	5	6

B7sus4	C7sus4	C#/Db7sus4	D7sus4	D#/Eb7sus4	E7sus4
7	8	9	10	11	12
7	8	9	10	11	12
9	10	11	12	13	14
7	8	9	10	11	12
9	10	11	12	13	14
7	8	9	10	11	12

Fifth string Root

13141

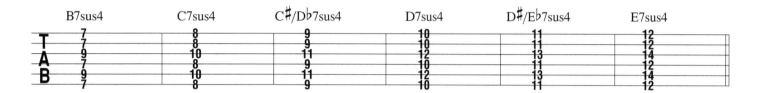

A#/Bb7sus4	B7sus4	C7sus4	C#/Db7sus4	D7sus4	D#/Eb7sus4
1	2	3	4	5	6
4	5	6	7	8	9
3	4	5	6	7	8
1	2	3	4	5	6

E7sus4	F7sus4	F#/Gb7sus4	G7sus4	G#/Ab7sus4	A7sus4
7	8	9	10	11	12
10	11	12	13	14	15
7	8	9	10	11	12
9	10	11	12	13	14
7	8	9	10	11	12

9

Sixth string Root

21314

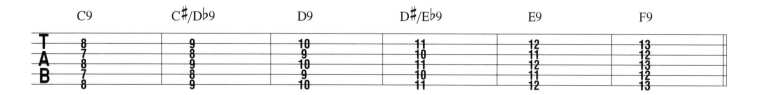

F#/Gb9	G9	G#/Ab9	A9	A#/Bb9	B9
2	3	4	5	6	7
1	2	3	4	5	6
2	3	4	5	6	7
1	2	3	4	5	6
2	3	4	5	6	7

C9	C#/Db9	D9	D#/Eb9	E9	F9
8	9	10	11	12	13
7	8	9	10	11	12
8	9	10	11	12	13
7	8	9	10	11	12
8	9	10	11	12	13

Fifth string Root

2 1 3 4

	B9	C9	C#/Db9	D9	D#/Eb9	E9
T	2	3	4	5	6	7
A	2	3	4	5	6	7
	1	2	3	4	5	6
B	2	3	4	5	6	7

	F9	F#/Gb9	G9	G#/Ab9	A9	A#/Bb9
T	8	9	10	11	12	13
A	8	9	10	11	12	13
	7	8	9	10	11	12
B	8	9	10	11	12	13

9sus4

Sixth string Root

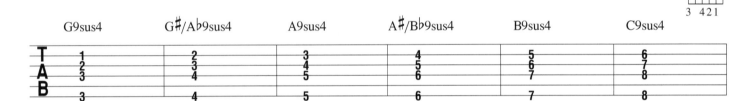

3 4 2 1

	G9sus4	G#/Ab9sus4	A9sus4	A#/Bb9sus4	B9sus4	C9sus4
T	1	2	3	4	5	6
A	2	3	4	5	6	7
	3	4	5	6	7	8
B	3	4	5	6	7	8

	C#/Db9sus4	D9sus4	D#/Eb9sus4	E9sus4	F9sus4	F#/Gb9sus4
T	7	8	9	10	11	12
A	8	9	10	11	12	13
	9	10	11	12	13	14
B	9	10	11	12	13	14

Fifth string Root

1 1 1 1

	A#/Bb9sus4	B9sus4	C9sus4	C#/Db9sus4	D9sus4	D#/Eb9sus4
T	1	2	3	4	5	6
A	1	2	3	4	5	6
	1	2	3	4	5	6
B	1	2	3	4	5	6

	E9sus4	F9sus4	F#/Gb9sus4	G9sus4	G#/Ab9sus4	A9sus4
T	7	8	9	10	11	12
A	7	8	9	10	11	12
	7	8	9	10	11	12
B	7	8	9	10	11	12

13

Sixth string Root

1 2 3 4

	F13	F#/Gb13	G13	G#/Ab13	A13	A#/Bb13
T	3	4	5	6	7	8
A	2	3	4	5	6	7
	1	2	3	4	5	6
B	1	2	3	4	5	6

	B13	C13	C#/Db13	D13	D#/Eb13	E13
T	9	10	11	12	13	14
A	8	9	10	11	12	13
	7	8	9	10	11	12
B	7	8	9	10	11	12

Fifth string Root

2 1 3 3 4

	B13	C13	C#/Db13	D13	D#/Eb13	E13
T	4	5	6	7	8	9
A	2	3	4	5	6	7
	2	3	4	5	6	7
	1	2	3	4	5	6
B	2	3	4	5	6	7

	F13	F#/Gb13	G13	G#/Ab13	A13	A#/Bb13
T	10	11	12	13	14	15
A	8	9	10	11	12	13
	8	9	10	11	12	13
	7	8	9	10	11	12
B	8	9	10	11	12	13

7#11

Sixth string Root

2 3 4 1

	F#/Gb7#11	G7#11	G#/Ab7#11	A7#11	A#/Bb7#11	B7#11
T	1	2	3	4	5	6
A	3	4	5	6	7	8
	2	3	4	5	6	7
B	2	3	4	5	6	7

	C7#11	C#/Db7#11	D7#11	D#/Eb7#11	E7#11	F7#11
T	7	8	9	10	11	12
A	9	10	11	12	13	14
	8	9	10	11	12	13
B	8	9	10	11	12	13

Fifth string Root

1 2 1 4

A#/Bb7#11	B7#11	C7#11	C#/Db7#11	D7#11	D#/Eb7#11
3	4	5	6	7	8
3	3	4	5	6	7
2	3	4	5	6	7
1	2	3	4	5	6

E7#11	F7#11	F#/Gb7#11	G7#11	G#/Ab7#11	A7#11
9	10	11	12	13	14
7	8	9	10	11	12
8	9	10	11	12	13
7	8	9	10	11	12

9#11

Sixth string Root

2 1 3 1 1

F#/Gb9#11	G9#11	G#/Ab9#11	A9#11	A#/Bb9#11	B9#11
1	2	3	4	5	6
1	2	3	4	5	6
2	3	4	5	6	7
1	2	3	4	5	6
2	3	4	5	6	7

C9#11	C#/Db9#11	D9#11	D#/Eb9#11	E9#11	F9#11
7	8	9	10	11	12
7	8	9	10	11	12
8	9	10	11	12	13
7	8	9	10	11	12
8	9	10	11	12	13

Fifth string Root

2 1 3 4 1

B9#11	C9#11	C#/Db9#11	D9#11	D#/Eb9#11	E9#11
1	2	3	4	5	6
2	3	4	5	6	7
2	3	4	5	6	7
1	2	3	4	5	6
2	3	4	5	6	7

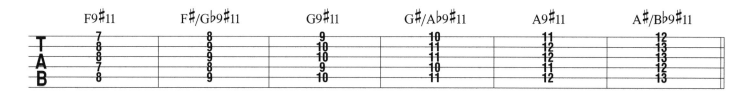

F9#11	F#/Gb9#11	G9#11	G#/Ab9#11	A9#11	A#/Bb9#11
7	8	9	10	11	12
8	9	10	11	12	13
8	9	10	11	12	13
7	8	9	10	11	12
8	9	10	11	12	13

13#11

Sixth string Root

F13#11	F#/G♭13#11	G13#11	G#/A♭13#11	A13#11	A#/B♭13#11
3	4	5	6	7	8
2	3	4	5	6	7
1	2	3	4	5	6
2	3	4	5	6	7
1	2	3	4	5	6

B13#11	C13#11	C#/D♭13#11	D13#11	D#/E♭13#11	E13#11
9	10	11	12	13	14
8	9	10	11	12	13
7	9	9	10	11	12
8	9	10	11	12	13
7	8	9	10	11	12

Fifth string Root

A#/B♭13#11	B13#11	C13#11	C#/D♭13#11	D13#11	D#/E♭13#11
3	4	5	6	7	8
3	4	5	6	7	8
1	2	3	4	5	6
2	3	4	5	6	7
1	2	3	4	5	6

E13#11	F13#11	F#/G♭13#11	G13#11	G#/A♭13#11	A13#11
9	10	11	12	13	14
9	10	11	12	13	14
7	8	9	10	11	12
8	9	10	11	12	13
7	8	9	10	11	12

7#5

Sixth string Root

F7#5	F#/G♭7#5	G7#5	G#/A♭7#5	A7#5	A#/B♭7#5
2	3	4	5	6	7
2	3	4	5	6	7
1	2	3	4	5	6
1	2	3	4	5	6

B7#5	C7#5	C#/D♭7#5	D7#5	D#/E♭7#5	E7#5
8	9	10	11	12	13
8	9	10	11	12	13
7	8	9	10	11	12
7	8	9	10	11	12

Fifth string Root

1413

	A#/Bb7#5	B7#5	C7#5	C#/Db7#5	D7#5	D#/Eb7#5
T	3	4	5	6	7	8
A	1	2	3	4	5	6
B	4	5	6	7	8	9
	1	2	3	4	5	6

	E7#5	F7#5	F#/Gb7#5	G7#5	G#/Ab7#5	A7#5
T	9	10	11	12	13	14
A	7	8	9	10	11	12
B	10	11	12	13	14	15
	7	8	9	10	11	12

9#5

Sixth string Root

1 2334

	F9#5	F#/Gb9#5	G9#5	G#/Ab9#5	A9#5	A#/Bb9#5
T	3	4	5	6	7	8
A	2	3	4	5	6	7
	2	3	4	5	6	7
	1	2	3	4	5	6
B	1	2	3	4	5	6

	B9#5	C9#5	C#/Db9#5	D9#5	D#/Eb9#5	E9#5
T	9	10	11	12	13	14
A	8	9	10	11	12	13
	8	9	10	11	12	13
	7	8	9	10	11	12
B	7	8	9	10	11	12

Fifth string Root

21334

	B9#5	C9#5	C#/Db9#5	D9#5	D#/Eb9#5	E9#5
T	3	4	5	6	7	8
A	2	3	4	5	6	7
	2	3	4	5	6	7
	1	2	3	4	5	6
B	2	3	4	5	6	7

	F9#5	F#/Gb9#5	G9#5	G#/Ab9#5	A9#5	A#/Bb9#5
T	9	10	11	12	13	14
A	8	9	10	11	12	13
	8	9	10	11	12	13
	7	8	9	10	11	12
B	8	9	10	11	12	13

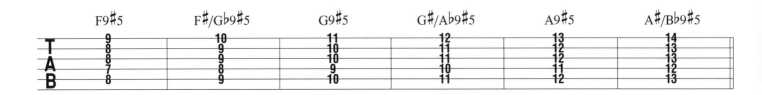

7♭9

Sixth string Root

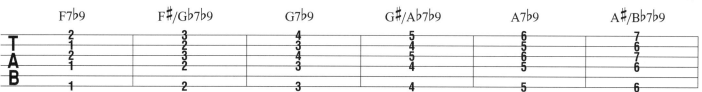

Fifth string Root

Fifth string Root

7♭9#5

Sixth string Root

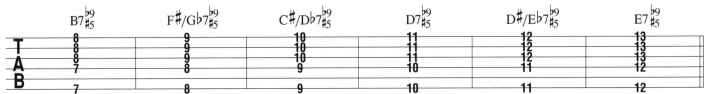

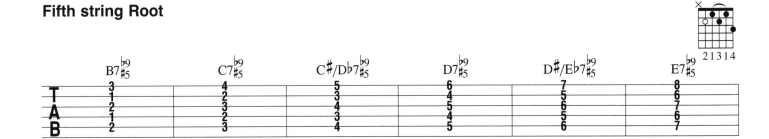

Fifth string Root

7♭9#11

Sixth string Root

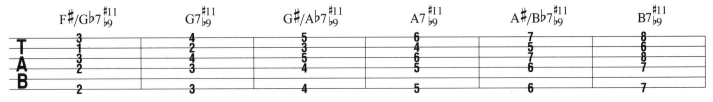

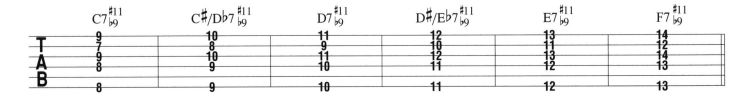

Fifth string Root

21311

	B7#11b9	C7#11b9	C#/Db7#11b9	D7#11b9	D#/Eb7#11b9	E7#11b9
	1	2	3	4	5	6
	1	2	3	4	5	6
	2	3	4	5	6	7
	1	2	3	4	5	6
	2	3	4	5	6	7

	F7#11b9	F#/Gb7#11b9	G7#11b9	G#/Ab7#11b9	A7#11b9	A#/Bb7#11b9
	7	8	9	10	11	12
	7	8	9	10	11	12
	8	9	10	11	12	13
	7	8	9	10	11	12
	8	9	10	11	12	13

13b9

Sixth string Root

1 1243

	F13b9	F#/Gb13b9	G13b9	G#/Ab13b9	A13b9	A#/Bb13b9
	2	3	4	5	6	7
	2	3	4	5	6	7
	2	3	4	5	6	7
	1	2	3	4	5	6
	1	2	3	4	5	6

	B13b9	C13b9	C#/Db13b9	D13b9	D#/Eb13b9	E13b9
	8	9	10	11	12	13
	9	10	11	12	13	14
	8	9	10	11	12	13
	7	8	9	10	11	12
	7	8	9	10	11	12

Fifth string Root

21314

	B13b9	C13b9	C#/Db13b9	D13b9	D#/Eb13b9	E13b9
	4	5	6	7	8	9
	1	2	3	4	5	6
	1	2	3	4	5	6
	1	2	3	4	5	6
	2	3	4	5	6	7

	F13b9	F#/Gb13b9	G13b9	G#/Ab13b9	A13b9	A#/Bb13b9
	10	11	12	13	14	15
	7	8	9	10	11	12
	8	9	10	11	12	13
	7	8	9	10	11	12
	8	9	10	11	12	13

7#9

Sixth string Root

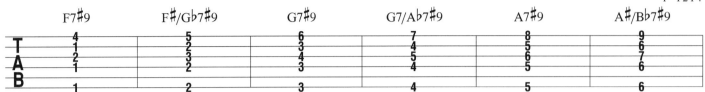

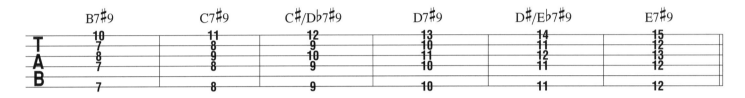

Fifth string Root

7#9#5

Sixth string Root

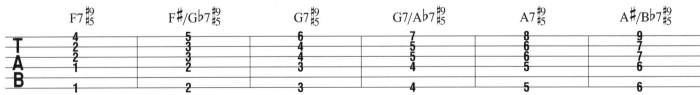

Fifth string Root

21344

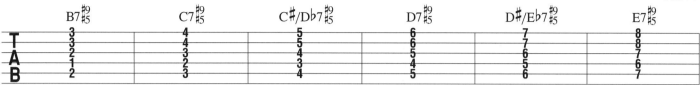

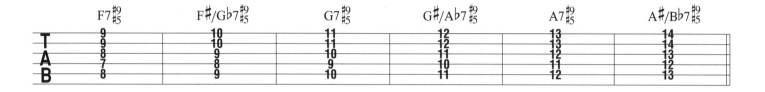

7♯9♯11

Sixth string Root

(T) 2314

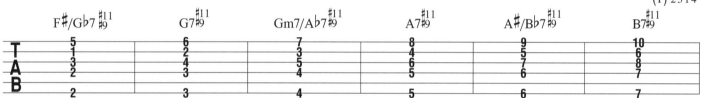

Fifth string Root

21341

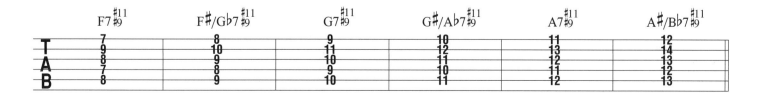

13#9

Sixth string Root

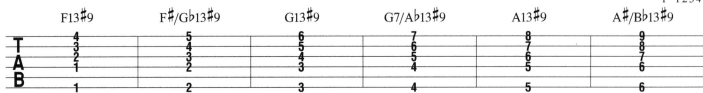

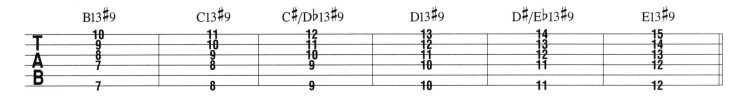

Minor Chords

Minor 7

Sixth string Root

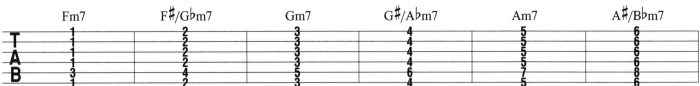

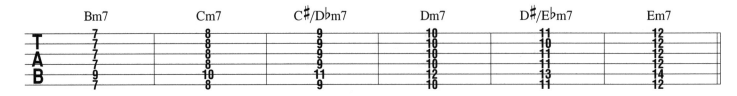

Fifth string Root

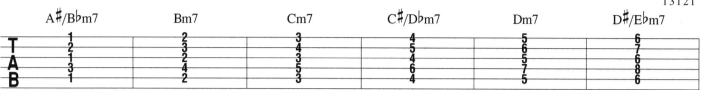

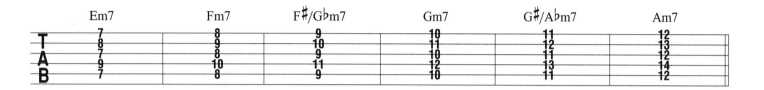

Fourth string Root

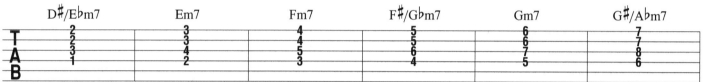

Minor 9

Sixth string Root

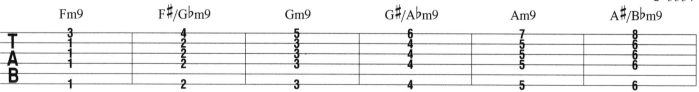

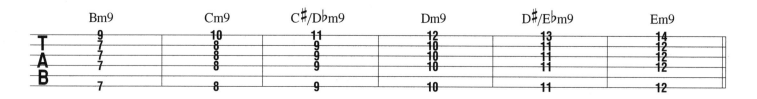

Fifth string Root

2 1 3 4

	Cm9	C#/Dbm9	Dm9	D#/Ebm9	Em9	Fm9
T	3	4	5	6	7	8
A	3	4	5	6	7	8
	1	2	3	4	5	6
B	3	4	5	6	7	8

	F#/Gbm9	Gm9	G#/Abm9	Am9	A#/Bbm9	Bm9
T	9	10	11	12	13	14
A	9	10	11	12	13	14
	7	8	9	10	11	12
B	9	10	11	12	13	14

Minor 11

Sixth string Root

2 3 4 1

	Gm11	G#/Abm11	Am11	A#/Bbm11	Bm11	Cm11
T	1	2	3	4	5	6
A	3	4	5	6	7	8
	3	4	5	6	7	8
B	3	4	5	6	7	8

	C#/Dbm11	Dm11	D#/Ebm11	Em11	Fm11	F#/Gbm11
T	7	8	9	10	11	12
A	9	10	11	12	13	14
	9	10	11	12	13	14
B	9	10	11	12	13	14

Fifth string Root

2 3 4 1

	Cm11	C#/Dbm11	Dm11	D#/Ebm11	Em11	Fm11
T	1	2	3	4	5	6
A	4	5	6	7	8	9
	3	4	5	6	7	8
B	3	4	5	6	7	8

	F#/Gbm11	Gm11	G#/Abm11	Am11	A#/Bbm11	Bm11
T	7	8	9	10	11	12
A	10	11	12	13	14	15
	9	10	11	12	13	14
B	9	10	11	12	13	14

Minor 13

Sixth string Root

Fm13	F#/G♭m13	Gm13	G#/A♭m13	Am13	A#/B♭m13
3	4	5	6	7	8
1	2	3	4	5	6
1	2	3	4	5	6
1	2	3	4	5	6

Bm13	Cm13	C#/D♭m13	Dm13	D#/E♭m13	Em13
9	10	11	12	13	14
7	8	9	10	11	12
7	8	9	10	11	12
7	8	9	10	11	12

Fifth string Root

A#/B♭m13	Bm13	Cm13	C#/D♭m13	Dm13	D#/E♭m13
3	4	5	6	7	8
2	3	4	5	6	7
1	2	3	4	5	6
1	2	3	4	5	6

Em13	Fm13	F#/G♭m13	Gm13	G#/A♭m13	Am13
9	10	11	12	13	14
8	9	10	11	12	13
7	8	9	10	11	12
7	8	9	10	11	12

Minor 7♯5

Sixth string Root

141111

Fm7♯5	F#/G♭m7♯5	Gm7♯5	G#/A♭m7♯5	Am7♯5	A#/B♭m7♯5
1	2	3	4	5	6
1	2	3	4	5	6
1	2	3	4	5	6
1	2	3	4	5	6
4	5	6	7	8	9
1	2	3	4	5	6

Bm7♯5	Cm7♯5	C#/D♭m7♯5	Dm7♯5	D#/E♭m7♯5	Em7♯5
7	8	9	10	11	12
7	8	9	10	11	12
7	8	9	10	11	12
7	8	9	10	11	12
10	11	12	13	14	15
7	8	9	10	11	12

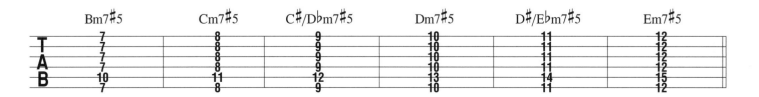

Fifth string Root

14 1 2 1

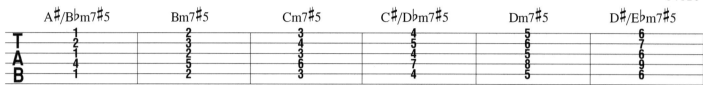

A#/Bbm7#5	Bm7#5	Cm7#5	C#/Dbm7#5	Dm7#5	D#/Ebm7#5

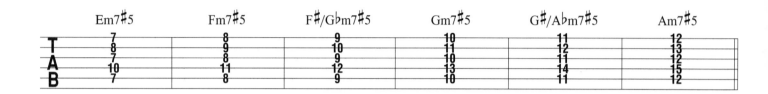

Em7#5	Fm7#5	F#/Gbm7#5	Gm7#5	G#/Abm7#5	Am7#5

Minor/maj7

Sixth string Root

1 3 2 1 1 1

Fm(maj7)	F#/Gbm(maj7)	Gm(maj7)	G#/Abm(maj7)	Am(maj7)	A#/Bbm(maj7)

Bm(maj7)	Cm(maj7)	C#/Dbm(maj7)	Dm(maj7)	D#/Ebm(maj7)	Em(maj7)

Fifth string Root

14 2 3 1

A#/Bbm(maj7)	Bm(maj7)	Cm(maj7)	C#/Dbm(maj7)	Dm(maj7)	D#/Ebm(maj7)

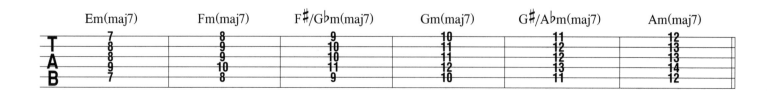

Em(maj7)	Fm(maj7)	F#/Gbm(maj7)	Gm(maj7)	G#/Abm(maj7)	Am(maj7)

Fifth string Root

4 2 1 1

C#/Dbm(maj7)	Dm(maj7)	D#/Ebm(maj7)	Em(maj7)	Fm(maj7)	F#/Gbm(maj7)
1	2	3	4	5	6
1	2	3	4	5	6
2	3	4	5	6	7
4	5	6	7	8	9

Bm(maj7)	Cm(maj7)	C#/Dbm(maj7)	Dm(maj7)	D#/Ebm(maj7)	Em(maj7)
7	8	9	10	11	12
7	8	9	10	11	12
8	9	10	11	12	13
10	11	12	13	14	15

Fourth string Root

1 3 4 2

D#/Ebm(maj7)	Em(maj7)	Fm(maj7)	F#/Gbm(maj7)	G#m(maj7)	G#/Abm(maj7)
2	3	4	5	6	7
3	4	5	6	7	8
3	4	5	6	7	8
1	2	3	4	5	6

Am(maj7)	A#/Bbm(maj7)	Bm(maj7)	Cm(maj7)	C#/Dbm(maj7)	Dm(maj7)
8	9	10	11	12	13
9	10	11	12	13	14
9	10	11	12	13	14
7	8	9	10	11	12

Minor/maj9

Sixth string Root

1 2 1 1 4

Fm(maj9)	F#/Gbm(maj9)	Gm(maj9)	G#/Abm(maj9)	Am(maj9)	A#/Bbm(maj9)
3	4	5	6	7	8
1	2	3	4	5	6
1	2	3	4	5	6
2	3	4	5	6	7
1	2	3	4	5	6

Bm(maj9)	Cm(maj9)	C#/Dbm(maj9)	Dm(maj9)	D#/Ebm(maj9)	Em(maj9)
9	10	11	12	13	14
7	8	9	10	11	12
7	8	9	10	11	12
8	9	10	11	12	13
7	8	9	10	11	12

Fifth string Root

2 1 4 3

	Cm(maj9)	C#/Dbm(maj9)	Dm(maj9)	D#/Ebm(maj9)	Em(maj9)	Fm(maj9)
T	3	4	5	6	7	8
	4	5	6	7	8	9
A	1	2	3	4	5	6
B	3	4	5	6	7	8

	F#/Gbm(maj9)	Gm(maj9)	G#/Abm(maj9)	Am(maj9)	A#/Bbm(maj9)	Bm(maj9)
T	9	10	11	12	13	14
	10	11	12	13	14	15
A	7	8	9	10	11	12
B	9	10	11	12	13	14

Minor 7♭5 Chords

Minor 7♭5

Sixth string Root

2 3 4 1

	F#m7b5	Gm7b5	G#/Abm7b5	Am7b5	A#/Bbm7b5	Bm7b5
T	1	2	3	4	5	6
	2	3	4	5	6	7
A	2	3	4	5	6	7
B	2	3	4	5	6	7

	Cm7b5	C#/Dbm7b5	Dm7b5	D#/Ebm7b5	Em7b5	Fm7b5
T	7	8	9	10	11	12
	8	9	10	11	12	13
A	8	9	10	11	12	13
B	8	9	10	11	12	13

Fifth string Root

1 3 2 4

	A#/Bbm7b5	Bm7b5	Cm7b5	C#/Dbm7b5	Dm7b5	D#/Ebm7b5
T	2	3	4	5	6	7
	1	2	3	4	5	6
A	2	3	4	5	6	7
B	1	2	3	4	5	6

	Em7b5	Fm7b5	F#/Gbm7b5	Gm7b5	G#/Abm7b5	Am7b5
T	8	9	10	11	12	13
	7	8	9	10	11	12
A	8	9	10	11	12	13
B	7	8	9	10	11	12

Fifth string Root

	Bm7♭5	Cm7♭5	C♯/D♭m7♭5	Dm7♭5	D♯/E♭m7♭5	Em7♭5
T	1	2	3	4	5	6
A	3	4	5	6	7	8
	2	3	4	5	6	7
B	2	3	4	5	6	7

	Fm7♭5	F♯/G♭m7♭5	Gm7♭5	G♯/A♭m7♭5	Am7♭5	A♯/B♭m7♭5
T	7	8	9	10	11	12
A	9	10	11	12	13	14
	8	9	10	11	12	13
B	8	9	10	11	12	13

Fourth string Root

	D♯/E♭m7♭5	Em7♭5	Fm7♭5	F♯m7♭5	Gm7♭5	G♯/A♭m7♭5
T	2	3	4	5	6	7
A	2	3	4	5	6	7
	2	3	4	5	6	7
B	1	2	3	4	5	6

	Am7♭5	A♯/B♭m7♭5	Bm7♭5	Cm7♭5	C♯/D♭m7♭5	Dm7♭5
T	8	9	10	11	12	13
A	8	9	10	11	12	13
	9	9	10	11	12	13
B	7	8	9	10	11	12

Dim7 Chords

Dim 7

Sixth string Root

	F♯/G♭°7	G°7	G♯/A♭°7	A°7	A♯/B♭°7	B°7
T	1	2	3	4	5	6
A	2	3	4	5	6	7
	1	2	3	4	5	6
B	2	3	4	5	6	7

	C°7	C♯/D♭°7	D°7	D♯/E♭°7	E°7	F°7
T	7	8	9	10	11	12
A	8	9	10	11	12	13
	7	8	9	10	11	12
B	8	9	10	11	12	13

Fifth string Root

2 3 1 4

	B°7	C°7	C#/Db°7	D°7	D#/Eb°7	E°7
T	3	4	5	6	7	8
A	1 3	2 4	3 5	4 6	5 7	6 8
B	3 2	4 3	5 4	6 5	7 6	8 7

	F°7	F#/Gb°7	G°7	G#/Ab°7	A°7	A#/Bb°7
T	9	10	11	12	13	14
A	7 9	8 10	9 11	10 12	11 13	12 14
B	9 8	10 9	11 10	12 11	13 12	14 13

Fifth string Root

2 1 4 1

	B°7	C°7	C#/Db°7	D°7	D#/Eb°7	E°7
T	1	2	3	4	5	6
A	3 1	4 2	5 3	6 4	7 5	8 6
B	2	3	4	5	6	7

	F°7	F#/Gb°7	G°7	G#/Ab°7	A°7	A#/Bb°7
T	7	8	9	10	11	12
A	9 7	10 8	11 9	12 10	13 11	14 12
B	8	9	10	11	12	13

Fourth string Root

1 3 2 4

	D#/Eb°7	E°7	F°7	F#/Gb°7	G°7	G#/Ab°7
T	2	3	4	5	6	7
A	1 2	2 3	3 4	4 5	5 6	6 7
B	1	2	3	4	5	6

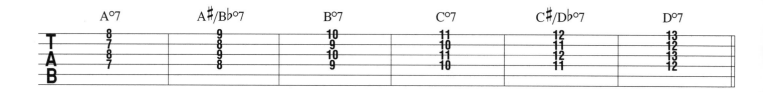

	A°7	A#/Bb°7	B°7	C°7	C#/Db°7	D°7
T	8	9	10	11	12	13
A	7 8	8 9	9 10	10 11	11 12	12 13
B	7	8	9	10	11	12

Music Examples

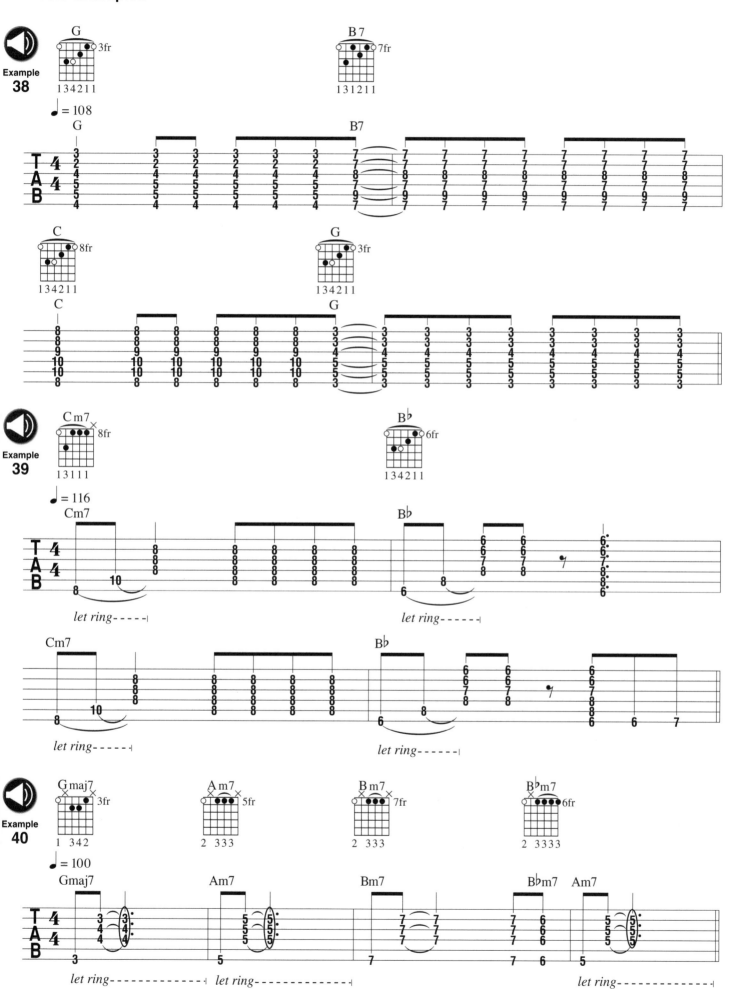

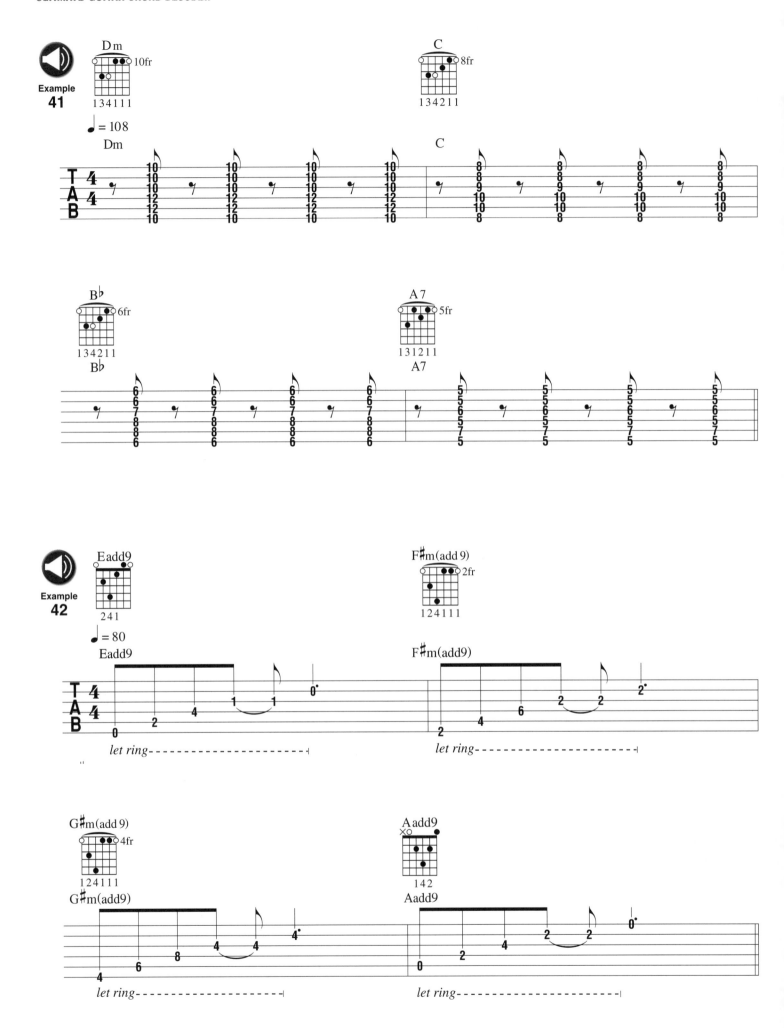

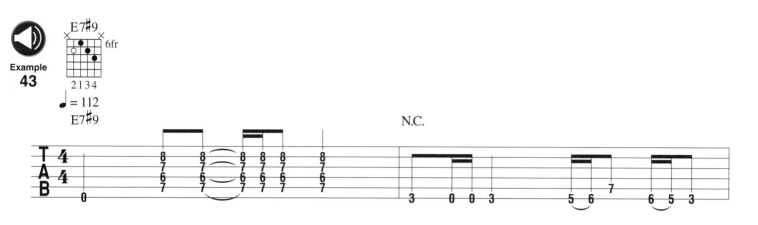

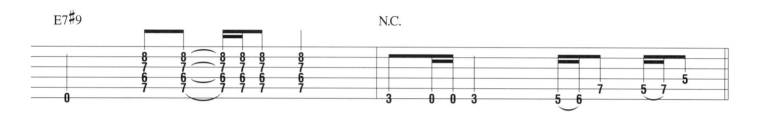

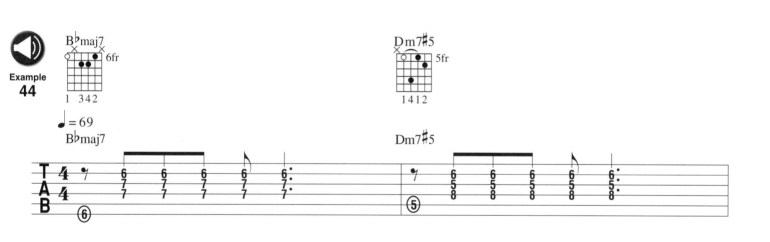

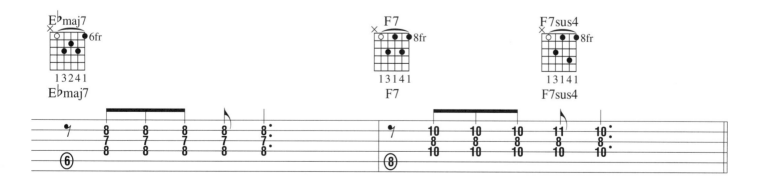

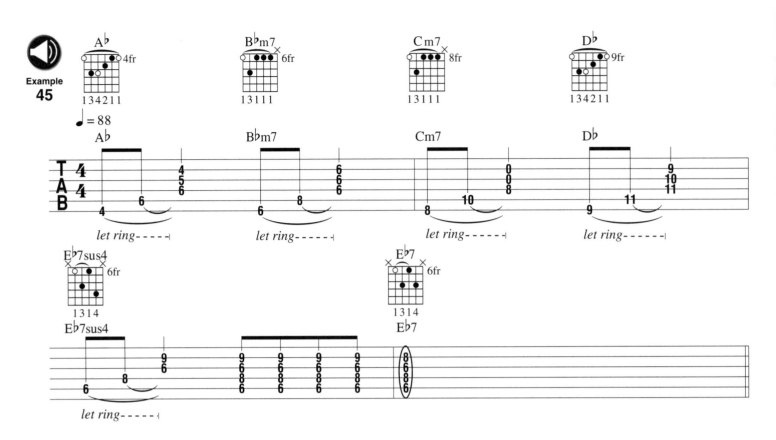

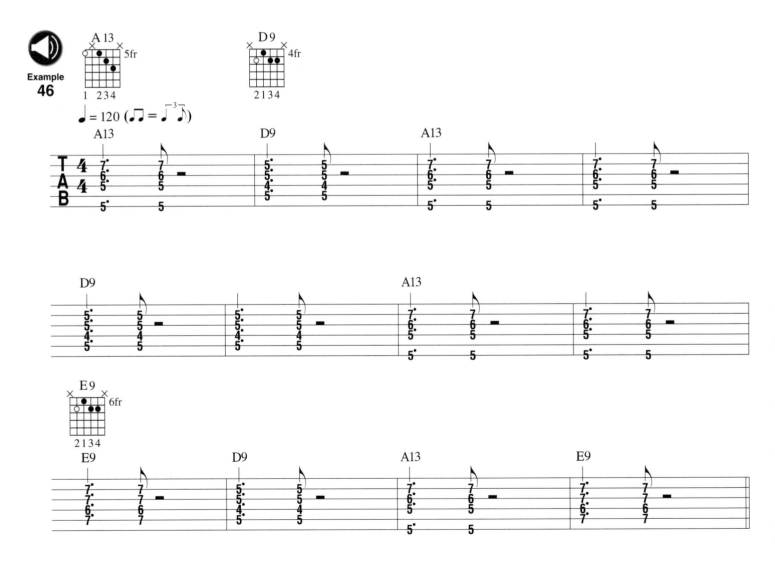

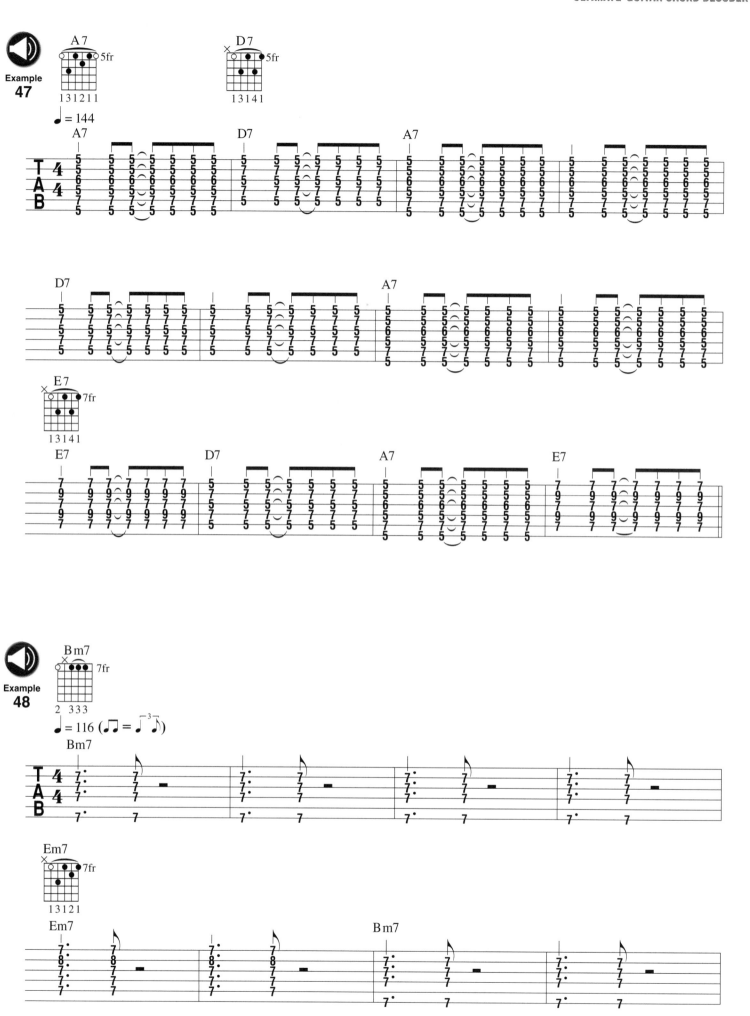

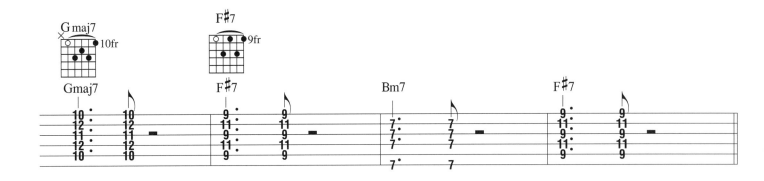

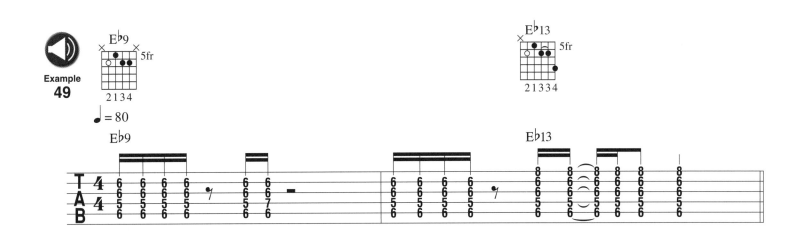

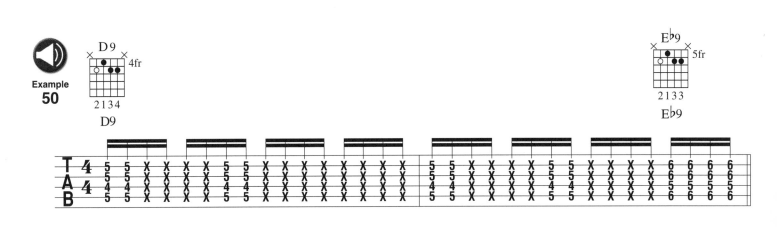

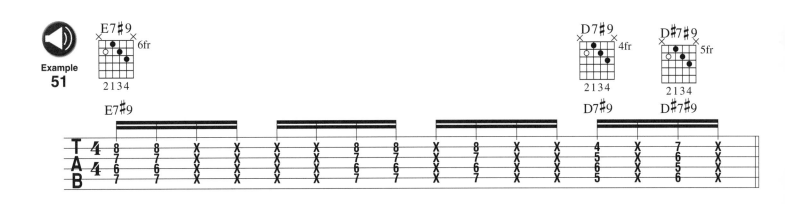

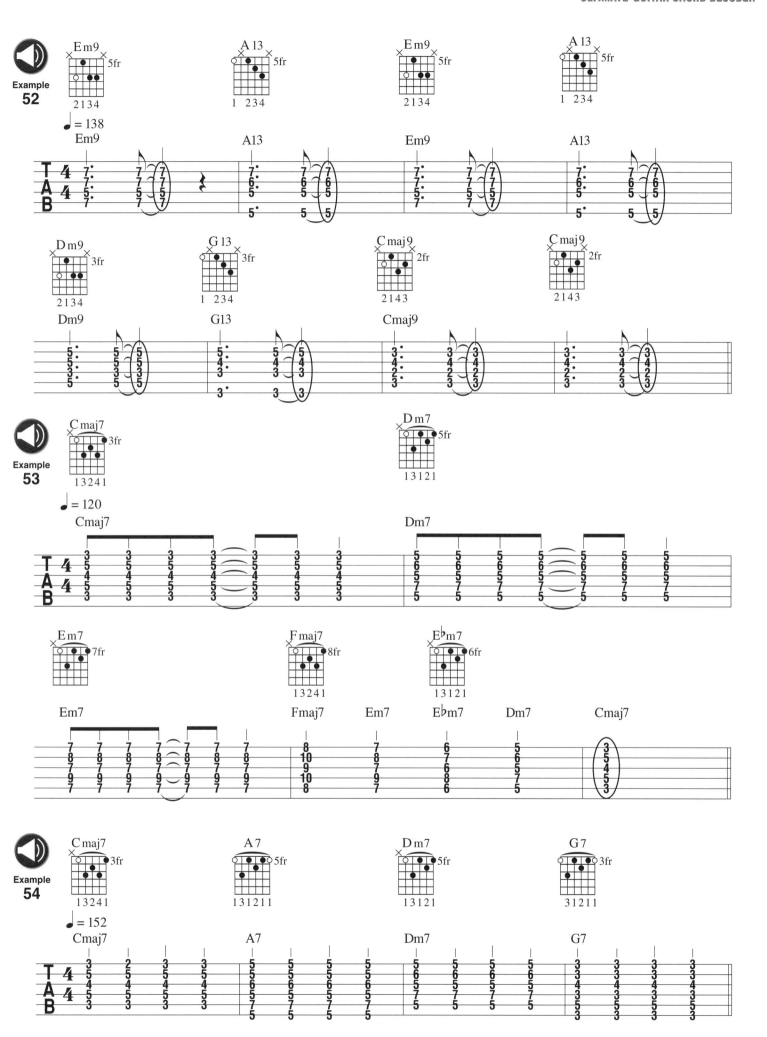

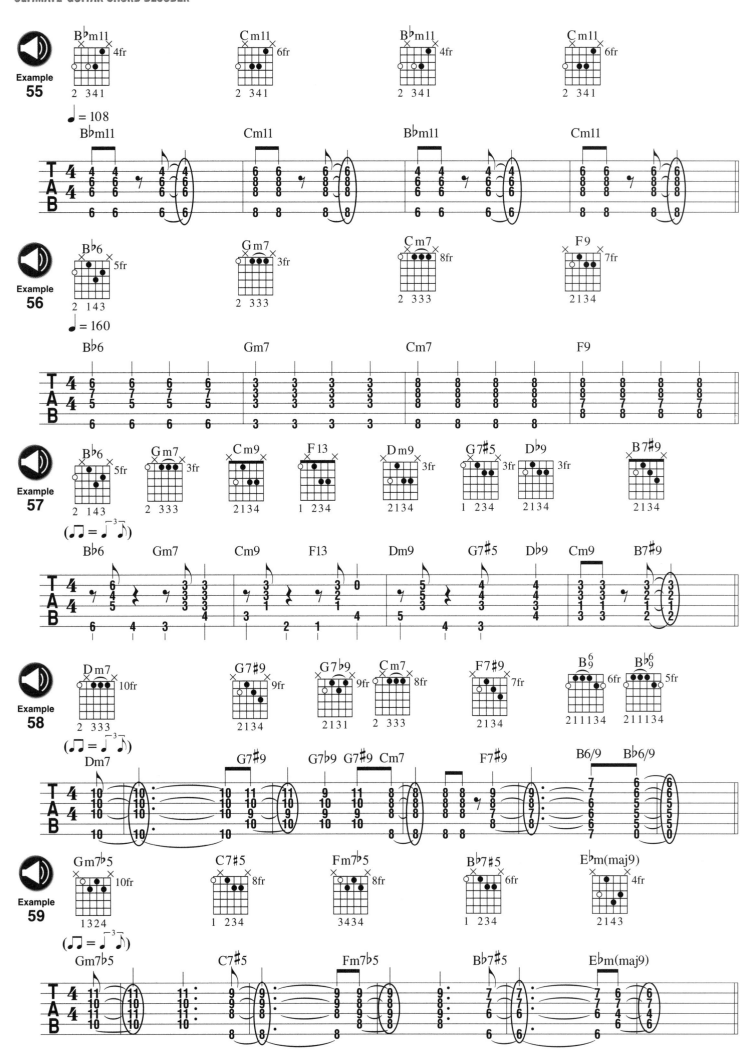

TRIADS AND INVERSIONS

We looked earlier at barre chord versions of triads. Sometimes, only a small fragment of a barre chord shape is used. You'll hear these abbreviated shapes used by guitarists like Eddie Van Halen in his inventive rhythm playing.

If you play only strings 4–3–2 of a sixth string A barre chord,

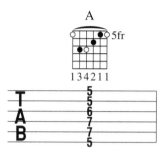

you get this shape:

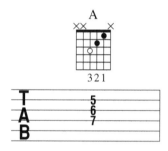

If you play only strings 3–2–1 of the same A barre chord, you get this shape:

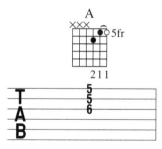

Can you see how these smaller fragments are derived from the full barre chord?

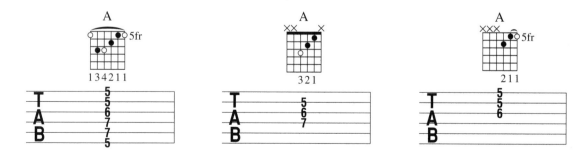

While chord fragments can be played on any set of strings, two of the most commonly used groupings are strings 4–3–2 and 3–2–1. The chord shapes that follow show major and minor triad fragments using these string sets. They are displayed with all three possible *inversions*. In case you aren't familiar with that term, inversions simply take the notes of a chord and rearrange them so a different note is on the bottom (the lowest string). Here are the three possible inversions of an A chord:

Root Position: A–C#–E
First Inversion: C#–E–A
Second Inversion: E–A–C#

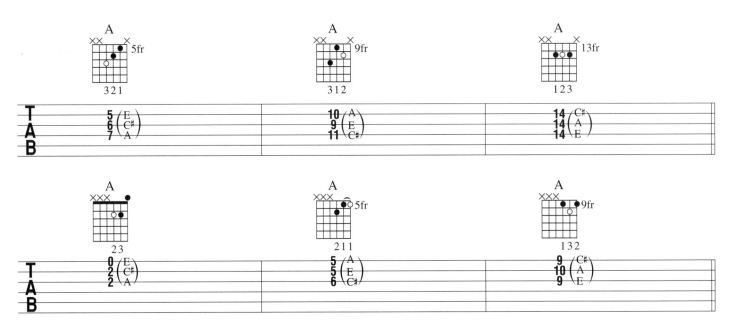

Major

Strings 4–3–2

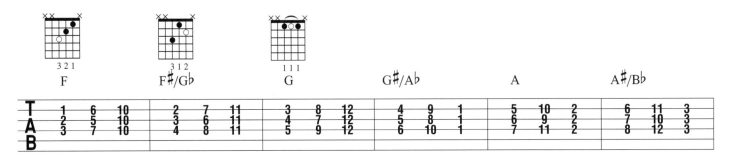

Strings 3–2–1

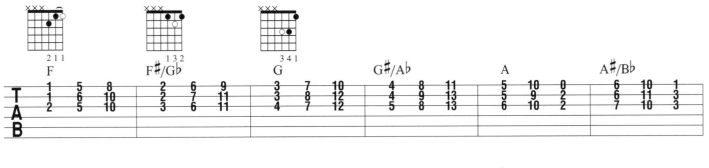

F	F#/Gb	G	G#/Ab	A	A#/Bb
1 5 8	2 6 9	3 7 10	4 8 11	5 10 0	6 10 1
1 6 10	2 7 11	3 8 12	4 9 13	5 9 2	6 11 3
2 5 10	3 6 11	4 7 12	5 8 13	6 10 2	7 10 3

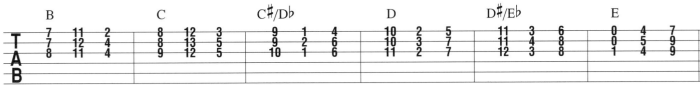

B	C	C#/Db	D	D#/Eb	E
7 11 2	8 12 3	9 1 4	10 2 5	11 3 6	0 4 7
7 12 4	8 13 5	9 2 6	10 3 7	11 4 8	0 5 9
8 11 4	9 12 5	10 1 6	11 2 7	12 3 8	1 4 9

Minor

Strings 4–3–2

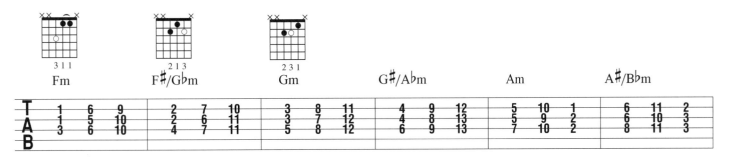

Fm	F#/Gbm	Gm	G#/Abm	Am	A#/Bbm
1 6 9	2 7 10	3 8 11	4 9 12	5 10 1	6 11 2
1 5 10	2 6 11	3 7 12	4 8 13	5 9 2	6 10 3
3 6 10	4 7 11	5 8 12	6 9 13	7 10 2	8 11 3

Bm	Cm	C#/Dbm	Dm	D#/Ebm	Em
7 12 3	8 13 4	9 2 5	10 3 6	11 4 7	0 5 8
7 11 4	8 12 5	9 1 6	10 2 7	11 3 8	0 4 9
9 12 4	10 13 5	11 2 6	12 3 7	13 4 8	2 5 9

Strings 3–2–1

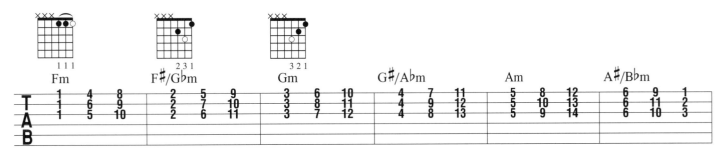

Fm	F#/Gbm	Gm	G#/Abm	Am	A#/Bbm
1 4 8	2 5 9	3 6 10	4 7 11	5 8 12	6 9 1
1 6 9	2 7 10	3 8 11	4 9 12	5 10 13	6 11 2
1 5 10	2 6 11	3 7 12	4 8 13	5 9 14	6 10 3

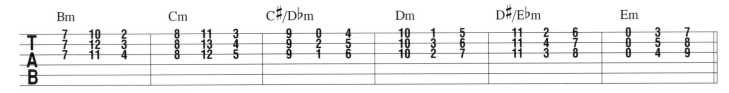

Bm	Cm	C#/Dbm	Dm	D#/Ebm	Em
7 10 2	8 11 3	9 0 4	10 1 5	11 2 6	0 3 7
7 12 3	8 13 4	9 2 5	10 3 6	11 4 7	0 5 8
7 11 4	8 12 5	9 1 6	10 2 7	11 3 8	0 4 9

Music Examples

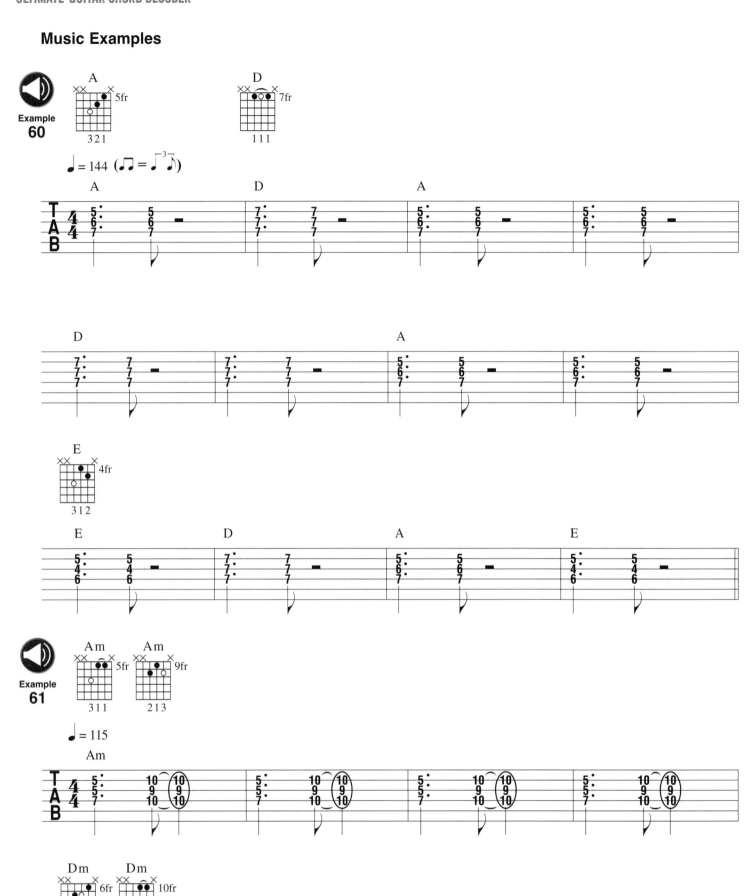

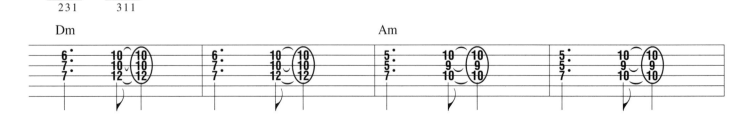

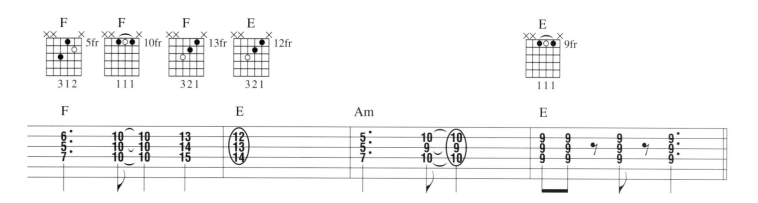

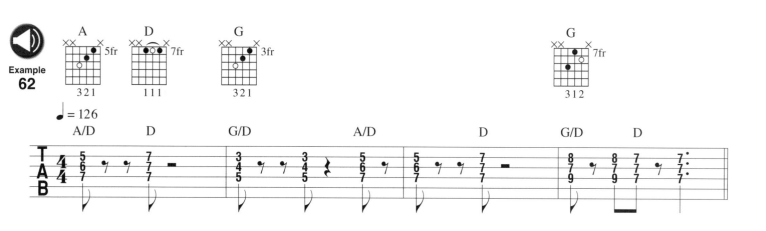

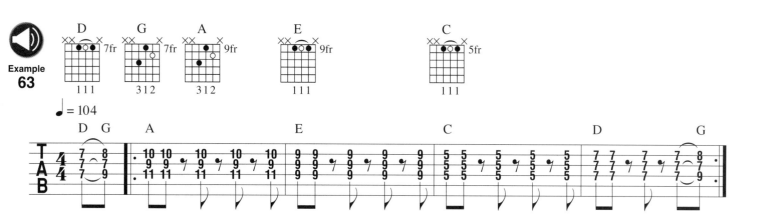

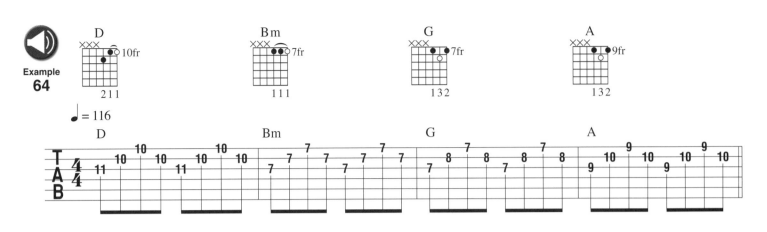

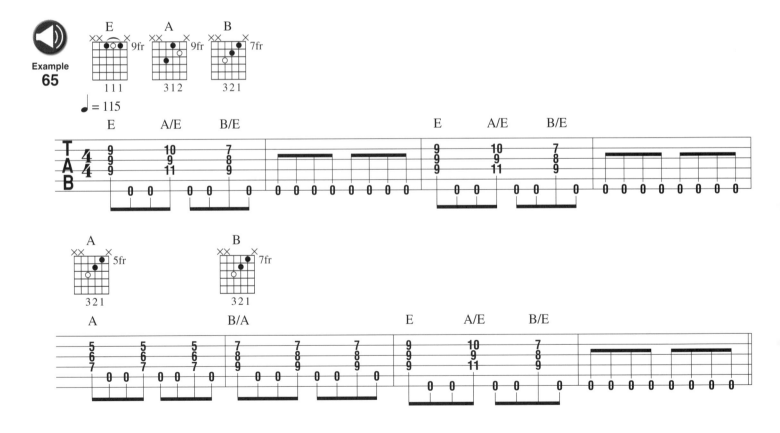

CHORD FORMULA CHART

CHORD NAME	FORMULA
major	1 3 5
minor	1 ♭3 5
sus4	1 4 5
sus2	1 2 5
augmented	1 3 ♯5
diminished	1 ♭3 ♭5
add9	1 3 5 9
madd9	1 ♭3 5 9
6	1 3 5 6
m6	1 ♭3 5 6
6/9	1 3 5 6 9
m6/9	1 ♭3 5 6 9
maj7	1 3 5 7
maj7♯11	1 3 5 7 (9) ♯11
maj9	1 3 5 7 9
maj9♯11	1 3 5 7 9 ♯11
maj13	1 3 5 7 9 13
maj7♯5	1 3 ♯5 7
7	1 3 5 ♭7
7sus4	1 4 5 ♭7
9	1 3 5 ♭7 9
11	1 3 5 ♭7 9 11
13	1 3 5 ♭7 9 (11) 13
9sus4	1 4 5 ♭7 9
13sus4	1 4 5 ♭7 9 13
7♯11	1 3 5 ♭7 ♯11
9♯11	1 3 5 ♭7 9 ♯11

CHORD NAME	FORMULA
13#11	1 3 5 ♭7 9 #11 13
7#5	1 3 #5 ♭7
9#5	1 3 #5 ♭7 9
7♭9	1 3 5 ♭7 ♭9
7♭9#5	1 3 #5 ♭7 ♭9
7♭9#11	1 3 #5 ♭7 ♭9 #11
13♭9	1 3 5 ♭7 ♭9 (#11) 13
7#9#5	1 3 #5 ♭7 #9
7#9#11	1 3 5 ♭7 #9 #11
13#9	1 3 5 ♭7 #9 (#11) 13
m(maj7)	1 ♭3 5 7
m(maj9)	1 ♭3 5 7 9
m7♭5	1 ♭3 ♭5 ♭7
dim7	1 ♭3 ♭5 ♭♭7

Get Better at Guitar

...with these Great Guitar Instruction Books from Hal Leonard!

101 GUITAR TIPS
INCLUDES TAB

STUFF ALL THE PROS KNOW AND USE

by Adam St. James

This book contains invaluable guidance on everything from scales and music theory to truss rod adjustments, proper recording studio set-ups, and much more. The book also features snippets of advice from some of the most celebrated guitarists and producers in the music business, including B.B. King, Steve Vai, Joe Satriani, Warren Haynes, Laurence Juber, Pete Anderson, Tom Dowd and others, culled from the author's hundreds of interviews.

00695737 Book/CD Pack..........................$16.95

AMAZING PHRASING
INCLUDES TAB

50 WAYS TO IMPROVE YOUR IMPROVISATIONAL SKILLS

by Tom Kolb

This book/CD pack explores all the main components necessary for crafting well-balanced rhythmic and melodic phrases. It also explains how these phrases are put together to form cohesive solos. Many styles are covered – rock, blues, jazz, fusion, country, Latin, funk and more – and all of the concepts are backed up with musical examples. The companion CD contains 89 demos for listening, and most tracks feature full-band backing.

00695583 Book/CD Pack..........................$19.95

BLUES YOU CAN USE
INCLUDES TAB

by John Ganapes

A comprehensive source designed to help guitarists develop both lead and rhythm playing. Covers: Texas, Delta, R&B, early rock and roll, gospel, blues/rock and more. Includes: 21 complete solos • chord progressions and riffs • turnarounds • moveable scales and more. CD features leads and full band backing.

00695007 Book/CD Pack..........................$19.95

FRETBOARD MASTERY
INCLUDES TAB

by Troy Stetina

Untangle the mysterious regions of the guitar fretboard and unlock your potential. *Fretboard Mastery* familiarizes you with all the shapes you need to know by applying them in real musical examples, thereby reinforcing and reaffirming your newfound knowledge. The result is a much higher level of comprehension and retention.

00695331 Book/CD Pack..........................$19.95

FRETBOARD ROADMAPS – 2ND EDITION

ESSENTIAL GUITAR PATTERNS THAT ALL THE PROS KNOW AND USE

by Fred Sokolow

The updated edition of this bestseller features more songs, updated lessons, and a full audio CD! Learn to play lead and rhythm anywhere on the fretboard, in any key; play a variety of lead guitar styles; play chords and progressions anywhere on the fretboard; expand your chord vocabulary; and learn to think musically – the way the pros do.

00695941 Book/CD Pack..........................$14.95

GUITAR AEROBICS
INCLUDES TAB

A 52-WEEK, ONE-LICK-PER-DAY WORKOUT PROGRAM FOR DEVELOPING, IMPROVING & MAINTAINING GUITAR TECHNIQUE

by Troy Nelson

From the former editor of *Guitar One* magazine, here is a daily dose of vitamins to keep your chops fine tuned! Musical styles include rock, blues, jazz, metal, country, and funk. Techniques taught include alternate picking, arpeggios, sweep picking, string skipping, legato, string bending, and rhythm guitar. These exercises will increase speed, and improve dexterity and pick- and fret-hand accuracy. The accompanying CD includes all 365 workout licks plus play-along grooves in every style at eight different metronome settings.

00695946 Book/CD Pack..........................$19.99

GUITAR CLUES
INCLUDES TAB

OPERATION PENTATONIC

by Greg Koch

Join renowned guitar master Greg Koch as he clues you in to a wide variety of fun and valuable pentatonic scale applications. Whether you're new to improvising or have been doing it for a while, this book/CD pack will provide loads of delicious licks and tricks that you can use right away, from volume swells and chicken pickin' to intervallic and chordal ideas. The CD includes 65 demo and play-along tracks.

00695827 Book/CD Pack..........................$19.95

INTRODUCTION TO GUITAR TONE & EFFECTS

by David M. Brewster

This book/CD pack teaches the basics of guitar tones and effects, with audio examples on CD. Readers will learn about: overdrive, distortion and fuzz • using equalizers • modulation effects • reverb and delay • multi-effect processors • and more.

00695766 Book/CD Pack..........................$14.99

PICTURE CHORD ENCYCLOPEDIA

This comprehensive guitar chord resource for all playing styles and levels features five voicings of 44 chord qualities for all twelve keys – 2,640 chords in all! For each, there is a clearly illustrated chord frame, as well as *an actual photo* of the chord being played! Includes info on basic fingering principles, open chords and barre chords, partial chords and broken-set forms, and more.

00695224..........................$19.95

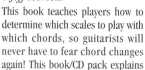

SCALE CHORD RELATIONSHIPS
INCLUDES TAB

by Michael Mueller & Jeff Schroedl

This book teaches players how to determine which scales to play with which chords, so guitarists will never have to fear chord changes again! This book/CD pack explains how to: recognize keys • analyze chord progressions • use the modes • play over nondiatonic harmony • use harmonic and melodic minor scales • use symmetrical scales such as chromatic, whole-tone and diminished scales • incorporate exotic scales such as Hungarian major and Gypsy minor • and much more!

00695563 Book/CD Pack..........................$14.95

SPEED MECHANICS FOR LEAD GUITAR
INCLUDES TAB

Take your playing to the stratosphere with the most advanced lead book by this proven heavy metal author. *Speed Mechanics* is the ultimate technique book for developing the kind of speed and precision in today's explosive playing styles. Learn the fastest ways to achieve speed and control, secrets to make your practice time really count, and how to open your ears and make your musical ideas more solid and tangible. Packed with over 200 vicious exercises including Troy's scorching version of "Flight of the Bumblebee." Music and examples demonstrated on CD. 89-minute audio.

00699323 Book/CD Pack..........................$19.95

TOTAL ROCK GUITAR
INCLUDES TAB

A COMPLETE GUIDE TO LEARNING ROCK GUITAR

by Troy Stetina

This unique and comprehensive source for learning rock guitar is designed to develop both lead and rhythm playing. It covers: getting a tone that rocks • open chords, power chords and barre chords • riffs, scales and licks • string bending, strumming, palm muting, harmonics and alternate picking • all rock styles • and much more. The examples are in standard notation with chord grids and tab, and the CD includes full-band backing for all 22 songs.

00695246 Book/CD Pack..........................$19.99

1013

HAL·LEONARD GUITAR PLAY-ALONG

INCLUDES TAB

This series will help you play your favorite songs quickly and easily. Just follow the tab and listen to the CD to hear how the guitar should sound, and then play along using the separate backing tracks. Mac or PC users can also slow down the tempo without changing pitch by using the CD in their computer. The melody and lyrics are included in the book so that you can sing or simply follow along.